A KIPLING CHRONOLOGY

Macmillan Author Chronologies

General Editor: Norman Page
Professor of Modern English Literature,
University of Nottingham

Reginald Berry
A POPE CHRONOLOGY

Edward Bishop
A VIRGINIA WOOLF CHRONOLOGY

Timothy Hands
A GEORGE ELIOT CHRONOLOGY

Owen Knowles
A CONRAD CHRONOLOGY

Harold Orel
A KIPLING CHRONOLOGY

Norman Page
A BYRON CHRONOLOGY
A DICKENS CHRONOLOGY
A DR JOHNSON CHRONOLOGY

F. B. Pinion
A WORDSWORTH CHRONOLOGY
A TENNYSON CHRONOLOGY

R. C. Terry
A TROLLOPE CHRONOLOGY

Further titles in preparation

A Kipling Chronology

HAROLD OREL

MACMILLAN

First published 1990

Published by
THE MACMILLAN PRESS LTD
Houndmills, Basingstoke, Hampshire RG21 2XS
and London
Companies and representatives
throughout the world

Typeset by Matrix
21, Russell St, London WC2

Printed in Hong Kong

British Cataloguing in Publication Data
Orel, Harold, 1926–
A Kipling chronology.—(Macmillan author
chronologies)
1. English literature. Kipling, Rudyard,
1865–1936. Biographies
I. Title
828′.809
ISBN 0-333-45915-6

To Larry and Joan McCaffrey

Contents

General Editor's Preface

Most biographies are ill adapted to serve as works of reference – not surprisingly so, since the biographer is likely to regard his function as the devising of a continuous and readable narrative, with excursions into interpretation and speculation, rather than a bald recital of facts. There are times, however, when anyone reading for business or pleasure needs to check a point quickly or to obtain a rapid overview of part of an author's life or career; and at such moments turning over the pages of a biography can be a time-consuming and frustrating occupation. The present series of volumes aims at providing a means whereby the chronological facts of an author's life and career, rather than needing to be prised out of the narrative in which they are (if they appear at all) securely embedded, can be seen at a glance. Moreover, whereas biographies are often, and quite understandably, vague over matters of fact (since it makes for tediousness to be for ever enumerating details of dates and places), a chronology can be precise whenever it is possible to be precise.

Thanks to the survival, sometimes in very large quantities, of letters, diaries, notebooks and other documents, as well as to thoroughly researched biographies and bibliographies, this material now exists in abundance for many major authors. In the case of, for example, Dickens, we can often ascertain what he was doing in each month and week, and almost on each day, of his prodigiously active working life; and the student of, say, *David Copperfield* is likely to find it fascinating as well as useful to know just when Dickens was at work on each part of that novel, what other literary enterprises he was engaged in at the same time, whom he was meeting, what places he was visiting, and what were the relevant circumstances of his personal and professional life. Such a chronology is not, of course, a substitute for a biography; but its arrangement, in combination with its index, makes it a much more convenient tool for this kind of purpose; and it may be acceptable as a form of 'alternative' biography, with its own distinctive advantages as well as its obvious limitations.

Since information relating to an author's early years is usually scanty and chronologically imprecise, the opening section of some volumes in this series groups together the years of childhood and adolescence. Thereafter each year, and usually each month, is dealt with separately. Information not readily assignable to a specific month or day is given as a general note under the relevant year or month. Each volume also contains a bibliography of the principal sources of information. In the chronology itself, the sources of many of the more specific items, including quotations, are identified, in order that the reader who wishes to do so may consult the original contexts.

NORMAN PAGE

Introduction

Preparing an Author Chronology for Rudyard Kipling is a more complicated task than compiling one for an author who, from choice or because of limited funds (or whatever reason might apply), travelled moderately, moved quietly within a narrow circle of acquaintances, and maintained relatively uncomplicated relationships with a very small number of publishers. Kipling wrote about an unusually large number of visits to foreign countries, including, very close to the end of his life, Brazil; of his fellow professionals, only H. Rider Haggard comes close to matching him in the number of journeys made to far-flung corners of the globe. Kipling met and cultivated close friendships with scores of world leaders. And because of the cheap paper editions of Kipling's works, his widespread popularity throughout the world, and the absence of copyright protection in the United States, his publications have 'a more interesting and tortuous history than those of any other contemporary author'.*

I have tried to identify, factually and in as straightforward a manner as possible, key happenings in Kipling's life that help to explain the richness of his subject matter and the wide range of his allusions. It should be made clear, from the outset, that Kipling's posthumously published memoir, *Something of Myself*, valuable though it is as a final statement (for example, about the way in which he inked out words and sentences in successive drafts of his stories), is vague on dates; it is surprisingly incomplete as a record of key figures and events; and it sometimes offers us an inaccurate rendering of matters which we can check elsewhere. But, then, Kipling never had the time he needed to complete or edit the 'autobiography', such as it is, and perforce we must be satisfied to have it at all.

I have not deemed it necessary to identify every story in a collection, or to review the contents of individual volumes,

---

* A.W. Keats (ed.), in James McG. Stewart, *Rudyard Kipling: A Bibliographical Catalogue* (Toronto: Dalhousie University Press and University of Toronto Press, 1959) p. vi.

because such information is readily available elsewhere. However, major works are listed, year by year, as they came out. Important meetings and introductions are cited, though it would, for example, be tedious to list every encounter between Kipling and Cecil Rhodes, even if the information were available (and it is not). Moreover, because my emphasis is on Kipling as a creative artist, details of his restless travels in France, Belgium and Switzerland, travels that occupied fully two to six months of every year both before and after the First World War, have been kept to a minimum. Kipling's conscientious work for the Imperial War Graves Commission, the multiplying problems affecting the health of both Carrie and himself, and the speeches, banquets and honorary degrees of his final decades, have been viewed as less important, in this Chronology, than his earlier adventures and achievements. I believe that this emphasis is the one desired by most readers.

Only a few abbreviations are used, most notably RK for Rudyard Kipling, JLK for John Lockwood Kipling, and AMK for Alice Macdonald Kipling. Titles of books have always been spelled out. (Kipling wrote so many books that many readers would find it difficult to keep in mind what each set of initials might stand for.)

An Author Chronology, of course, can be very long indeed. At the University of Sussex, Brighton, four collections of Kipling materials are of particular interest to those who would like to accumulate additional materials for the study of Kipling's life: Kipling's own personal papers, the Baldwin Papers, the Carrington Papers, and the Hollings Collection of press cuttings. The first – the Kipling archive from Wimpole Hall – fills some 31 manuscript boxes, 16 × 11 × 4 inches, and the press cuttings take up 21 volumes (most of them of folio size). These collections also contain hundreds of letters on personal, social and literary matters; an edition of the letters to Kipling's children, 'O Beloved Kids', has been prepared and published by Elliot L. Gilbert (London: Weidenfeld and Nicolson, 1983), and Thomas Pinney is preparing a multi-volume edition of selected correspondence for Macmillan, to be published in the near future. The availability of these collections, recently opened to Kipling scholars, guarantees a continuing stream of publications that, inevitably, will modify our view of Kipling the man, and our understanding of what he accomplished. Also, there exist a number of other valuable collections of Kipling materials, such as the Doubleday Collection in the Princeton University Library; these deserve, and will get, fuller treatment than they have thus far received.

Here, in a convenient and (I hope) a readable format, is a chronicle of major events in Rudyard Kipling's life.

Acknowledgements

Special thanks are due to Professor Thomas Pinney, Pomona College, Claremont, California, for reading a manuscript draft of this book critically and sympathetically (though the responsibility for all errors and oversights remains with me, of course); to Professor Norman Page, Department of English Studies, University of Nottingham, for comradeship in Kipling matters (and much else); and to Frances Arnold, formerly an editor with the Macmillan Press, whose advice and support over the years have been much appreciated. This investigation was supported by University of Kansas General Research allocation no. 3064–XX–0038.

A Kipling Chronology

1865

30 December   RK is born in Bombay, six days after his mother's painful confinement begins. He is named Joseph (after his grandfather) and Rudyard (after the lake in Staffordshire, near Burslem, at which his parents had met during the spring of 1863). He is baptised in Bombay Cathedral; John Griffiths, assistant to his father, and his Aunt Louisa (by proxy), serve as sponsors.

RK's father, John Lockwood Kipling (born 1837), is the son of a Methodist minister, and began his working career in art in Burslem, designing dinner plates for Pinder, Bourne, a Wesleyan firm. He attended the local art school at Stoke. He joined Birnie Philip, a popular architectural sculptor in London. His work (beginning in 1861) on the construction of the new Museum of Art at South Kensington (later to be called the Victoria and Albert Museum) was mostly concerned with terracotta mosaic. He modelled from designs by his employer, Godfrey Sykes.

He wed Alice Macdonald (born 1837) at St Mary Abbot's Church, Kensington, on 18 March 1865. (Both were 28 years old.) Georgiana, Alice's sister, managed the arrangements. Frederick Macdonald gave his sister away. Shortly before the wedding, in 1864, JLK was appointed Professor of Architectural Sculpture in the Jeejeebhoy School of Art, Bombay, at a salary of 400 rupees (about £36) a month. Sir Philip Cunliffe-Owen had highly recommended him for the post.

Alice Macdonald, in the years before the wedding, had been engaged several times: once to William Allingham, a member of the Rossettis' circle, and twice to William Fulford, also in the Rossetti circle, and later ordained. John took Lockwood as his first name for professional reasons shortly before the wedding. This event was followed by a lavish reception, attended by Ford Madox Brown, Swinburne and the two Rossettis. JLK and AMK went to Ripton to visit JLK's family, and on 12 April sailed for India in the P & O ship *Ripon*, travelling overland across the Suez Peninsula.

JLK is one of three teachers appointed to instruct students in such utilitarian technical crafts as moulding, the manufacture

1

and design of terracotta pottery, and architectural sculpture. Working for poor pay, he is responsible for the artistic efforts of 20 pupils, and getting by will be something of a struggle.

1866

Georgiana Macdonald ('Aunt Georgie') has married Edward Burne-Jones in 1860. Agnes Macdonald ('Auntie Aggie') marries Sir Edward Poynter, President of the Royal Academy, and Louisa Macdonald ('Aunt Louie') marries Alfred Baldwin (their child, Stanley, will become Prime Minister, and afterwards the 1st Earl Baldwin of Bewdley).

1868

February AMK, knowing she is pregnant again, decides to have her child in England. Passengers from India at that time go overland from Suez to Alexandria, since the canal has not been completed. RK, less than two and a half years of age, will remember in later years that there was a train across the desert, and that it stopped because of a (false) alarm that the train was on fire. His father predicts that some day he will return 'in a big steamer'. RK behaves obnoxiously aboard ship.

10 March The Kiplings arrive in England. Alice and her son go to the village of Bewdley, Worcestershire, where her parents – George Browne Macdonald, a famous Wesleyan preacher, and Hannah, daughter of John Jones of Manchester – live in a three-storey house on the River Severn. RK sleeps in the same bed as his aunt Edith Macdonald; restless, he often kicks her during the night. The grandfather, George Macdonald, is old, ill, and impatient with 'Ruddy'. (Edith later claims that RK 'hastened and embittered' the last days of his grandfather, who dies murmuring, 'Lord, what things I lie here and remember.') Uncle Fred Macdonald writes to his brother in America that Rudyard loves JLK, but bullies AMK. Rudy 'is a power and a problem with strange gifts of upsetting any household'.

11 June AMK has a second dangerous confinement at the Burne-Joneses' home, The Grange, North End Road, Fulham. (The Grange was once the home of Samuel Richardson. Its present owner, Edward Burne-Jones, gives wonderful parties for Charles Faulkner, Edward Poynter, William de Morgan, May and Jenny Morris, William Morris, and many other artists, writers and intellectuals.) Alice, the new-born child, weighs 11 pounds, has a broken arm and black eye, and seems to be stillborn. The doctor whips her alive 'with a towel wrung out with ice water'. She acquires her nickname of 'Trixie' or 'Trix' from JLK's description of her as a 'tricksy baby'.

7 November The Kiplings leave England. Back in India RK becomes an unquestioned 'despot'. Because he speaks to the servants in their own language, he often has to be reminded to speak English in the dining-room. He loves his Hindu bearer and his ayah, a Roman Catholic from Goa (who takes charge of Trixie); Dunnoo, who tends the 'fat white pony' that RK calls Dapple Gray; and Chokra, the boy who calls the other servants.

1870

April A third child, John, is born, and dies. JLK secures a commission to send in news reports to the *Pioneer*, an English-language newspaper published in Allahabad. AMK runs the house, and writes for magazines and local newspapers. Her talents as a social hostess are widely recognised.

1871

15 April The Kiplings sail from Bombay on leave for eight months; they go to Suez and England on the P & O ship *Ripon*. Their aim: to have the children escape the fever-ridden climate of India and to acquire an English education. An advertisement placed by a retired merchant captain, Pryse Agar (Harry) Holloway, and his wife, Sarah, announces that they take in children whose parents are in India; they live in a detached house called Lorne Lodge (5 Campbell Road, Havelock Park) in Southsea, Hampshire. Holloway was a midshipman on *HMS Brisk* in 1825, and later

joined the merchant marine. The head of his family is General
(Sir) Thomas Holloway, his eldest brother, who lives at West
Lodge, Havant (which RK later will see). When he dies (July
1875), he leaves nothing to his nephew, Henry's son, though the
reason why he changed his mind remains unclear.

3 October RK is nearly six, Trix a little over three, when
their parents leave them with the Holloways. JLK and AMK
do not display undue emotion, and RK has no warning of
the impending separation. RK lives with the Holloways for five
years and three months, from the age of six until he reaches 11.
The nickname 'Punch' is lost, and he is renamed 'Black Sheep'.
Mrs Holloway, most likely a Calvinist Evangelical of the Church
of England, takes an increasing dislike to him; he in turn calls
her a '*Kuch-nay*, a Nothing-at-all', 'of such a low caste as not to
matter'. This bitterly unhappy period seems to have been an odd
and perhaps unnecessary change in the circumstances of RK's
life. Relatives on both sides of the family had offered homes to
the children. Grandmother Kipling, of whom Trix spoke with
affection, lived in Skipton, Yorkshire, and a daughter Ruth lived
nearby. Trix later will write that her grandmother should have
been chosen as her guardian. Three aunts – Louie (Baldwin),
Aggie (Poynter) and Georgie (Burne-Jones) – have young children
the same age as RK and Trix. Also, there once was a plan that RK
should divide his time equally between the Burne-Jones family and
his uncle Fred Macdonald. If this plan had gone into effect, he
would have spent his holidays with Trix for the five years that
his mother was away. But AMK insists that RK and Trix should
not be separated. JLK, a little younger than his wife, agrees.

1872

Harry Holloway likes RK, provides some protection for RK against
both his wife and their son (Henry Thomas Holloway); teaches RK
old sea-songs; and introduces him to Surtees' *Jorrocks*.

August–September The Macdonald grandmother (Hannah), accompanied by two of the aunts, comes down to Southsea to
visit RK and Trix. The relatives are satisfied with the general
condition of the children. Hannah writes, 'They seem much

attached to Mrs Holloway and she seems fond of them.' RK and the Holloways' son attend Hope House, Somerset Place, Green Street, as a day-school. Mr T. H. Vickerey is the principal. RK dislikes Hope House as not 'a proper place'.

1873

December   Possibly RK's first visit to the Grange. It is probably in this year that William Morris, playing the role of 'Uncle Topsy', sits on a rocking-horse and tells RK and little Margaret Burne-Jones the story of *Eyrbyggja Saga*.

1874

Harry Holloway takes RK on a visit to Oxford, a stop-over on the way to the Baldwins at Bewdley, and RK meets Edward Hawkins, the Provost of Oriel. (See 'The Brushwood Boy' for a recollection of this happy event.)

In this year RK finally masters the art of reading, after a long and difficult start.

20 September   Uncle Harry dies.

December   RK's second visit to the Grange.

1875

JLK moves from Bombay to Lahore, where he is appointed Principal of the New Mayo School of Art and Curator of the Museum. (The Bombay School of Art is taken over by John Griffiths.) JLK's promotion sets back by three years AMK's plan to return to England, delaying RK's removal from Lorne Lodge.

The Baldwins take a house in Albert Terrace (later to be called Albert Gate), London. Charles Reade once lived here, but it has deteriorated into a shabby place with unreliable sanitation; however, its view over Hyde Park is attractive.

December   Third visit to the Grange.

1876

Spring JLK falls sick, develops typhoid, and almost dies. AMK nurses him diligently and saves his life.

October RK visits either the *Alert* or the *Discovery*. The Arctic Expedition has returned to Portsmouth after spending the winter further north than any other ships thus far.

December Fourth visit to the Grange.

1877

1 January JLK designs 70 Chinese-satin banners for chieftains at a Delhi ceremony marking the Proclamation of Queen Victoria as Empress of India. (He has been working on them since Sep 1876.) He is rewarded with 500 rupees and a silver medal by the Indian Government.

Around this time, Aunt Georgie, alarmed by evidence of RK's rapidly deteriorating vision, writes to her sister in Lahore that she should return to England.

March AMK arrives at Southsea and rescues RK from Mrs Holloway and the oppressive atmosphere of Lorne Lodge. There are many family reunions, including visits to Yorkshire. She takes both children to Goldings Hill, a farm near Loughton, Essex, on the edge of Epping Forest. They ride ponies all summer. They play with Stan Baldwin, their cousin, and live with a family named Pinder (Pinder was JLK's chief in the Staffordshire potteries). Mr Dally, a farmer, provides guidelines for their behaviour on his farm. They are not to leave gates open, throw stones at the animals, or break down the orchard trees. They learn farm lore, and enjoy their conversations with 'Jarge', a farmboy who tells (and sometimes improvises) stories. RK participates in pig-killings; races hoops with Trix and Stan; rides donkeys (a gypsy named Saville supervises this); and celebrates Guy Fawkes Night with exuberance.

Autumn and Winter RK goes from Goldings Hill to a small lodging-house at 227 Brompton Road, London. The house is rented by an ex-butler and his wife. RK here first learns the pleasures of walking around at night. (He will write numerous poems and short stories about the pleasures and terrors of night-time activity.) During the day he and Trix throw down into the London street pieces of coal, or walnuts wrapped in paper, to watch well-dressed people in the street pick them up, unwrap them, and throw them away in disgust.

December AMK, about to leave for India, brings RK to the home of 'the Ladies of Warwick Gardens' (Trix has gone back to Southsea and Mrs Holloway). Two of these three women are daughters of Professor George Lillie Craik, an authority on English literature and language, and cousins of Sir Henry Craik. The third lady is Miss Winnard. Georgiana Craik, a minor novelist, her sister Mary, and Miss Winnard live near Addison Road, at 26 Warwick Gardens. RK stays with them a few weeks before he is scheduled to go to public school. He will remember the house as a place 'filled with books, peace, kindliness, patience and what today would be called "culture" '. (See W.L. Murray Brooks, 'A Note on Mrs Hooper', *Kipling Journal*, Sep 1960, pp. 15–16, which notes that the Ladies had a friend named Mrs George Hooper, née Wynnard; hence some confusion in a few biographies about a 'Mrs Winnard'.)

1878

At the beginning of the year RK, aged 12, starts at the United Services College, a public school founded in 1874. It is located in Westward Ho!, a village founded as a property speculation not long before USC itself. It overlooks Bideford Bay, north Devon. The objective of the school is to coach students for the Army Entrance Examination, specifically for admission to the training-colleges at Sandhurst and Woolwich. (Gladstone had abolished the purchase of commissions in the Army in 1871.) A row of lodging-houses – 'twelve bleak houses by the shore', RK will describe them later, more disparagingly than necessary – is united by a corridor that runs the whole length of the terrace. Three-quarters of the approximately 200 students have been born overseas, and their parents (mostly officers) do not have much money. Many of the students are 'problem boys' from other schools. At one end of USC is a gymnasium; at the other, the Headmaster's house. The Headmaster is Cormell Price, known to RK as 'Uncle Crom' because of his close friendships with Burne-Jones and others well-known to the Grange, such as Charles Eliot Norton (an American), the Rossettis, Holman Hunt, Ford Madox Brown, Swinburne, and William Morris. Uncle Crom has taught for 10 years at Haileybury, a top school for would-be Army officers; because he believes in the kind of education practised at Thomas Arnold's Rugby and because he is supported by a dedicated and humane faculty, the atmosphere of USC never becomes oppressively military, and the school is very different from most public schools. There is no organised fagging, and prefects are allowed to smoke. RK enters school wearing thick spectacles, and he is just beginning to grow a moustache. He goes straight into the Lower Third, Easter Term, and remains there until the end of Easter Term 1879. During his first term he meets George Beresford (later immortalised as M'Turk in *Stalky & Co.*), and is in the Lower Third. L.C. Dunsterville becomes an even closer friend than Beresford, and will be reincarnated, in fictional terms, as the great Stalky. RK calls himself 'Beetle'. His first great hate is the school chaplain, the Revd J.C. Campbell, who will leave in RK's second year.

AMK (who will remain in Europe till the autumn of 1880) is joined by JLK, who has earned eight months leave. One duty that he takes pleasure in fulfilling during this period, however, is organising the Indian section of Arts and Manufactures at the International Exposition in Paris. At the end of his first term, in the spring, RK accompanies him to Paris (they stay in a boarding-house 'at the back of the Parc Mon̨ceau'); enjoys sightseeing; enters the head of the unassembled Statue of Liberty, by Bartholdi (to be erected in New York Harbour in 1886); and is to claim, in later years, that this visit begins his lifelong love affair with France and French culture.

1879

Because of his poor sight, RK cannot join in organised games such as cricket and football. He studies Latin, especially the Third Book of Horace's *Odes*, English, French and Mathematics (in which he does poorly). He becomes an omnivorous reader.

His nickname of 'Giglamps' or 'Giggers', or even 'Gigs', comes from Robert Browning's Gigadibs, 'the literary man' in *Men and Women*, and alludes to his glasses. He enjoys American literature: Emerson (a special favourite), Lowell, Whitman, the American humorists, Poe, Longfellow, Twain, and Harris's Uncle Remus. In English literature he develops an affection for Hakluyt's *Voyages*; Defoe, Bunyan, Fielding, Smollett, Dickens and Thackeray; Ruskin's *Fors Clavigera* and Carlyle's *Sartor Resartus*; pre-eminently Browning; Landor's *Imaginary Conversations*; Borrow's *Lavengro* and FitzGerald's *Rubáiyát*; Donne, Peacock, and Swinburne's *Atlanta in Calydon*. He also reads Pushkin and Lermontov (in French translation).

In this year he begins writing poems and fragments of poems which are never to get into the Definitive Edition. Between 1879 and 1882 at USC, and between 1882 and 1889, when he serves as a journalist in Lahore and Allahabad, he is to write at least 300 such poems, so far as the record goes.

June RK's first known story, 'My First Adventure', is published in *The Scribbler*, a family magazine worked on with the Burne-Jones and Morris children. RK uses the pen-name 'Nickson'.

After being prepared by the Revd G. Willes ('Gillett' in *Stalky & Co.*), RK is confirmed in Bideford Church by the Bishop of Exeter.

Summer and Autumn Terms RK is in the Upper Third.

1880

In this and subsequent years, RK visits Warwick Gardens as often as possible. There he meets Gilbert Murray.

Spring AMK nurses RK through a minor illness (quinsy).

RK acts in a student version of *Aladdin and the Wonderful Lamp*, by John Maddison Morton (1856); it is renamed *Aladdin, or the Wonderful Scamp*. He plays Widow Twanky; Dunsterville, the Sultan; and Beresford, the 'obscure character of the Executioner'. (Beresford, 54 years later, says that he played Widow Twanky, and RK the Executioner; RK's memory of the event, however, was probably more accurate, being closer in time – only 16 years after the production.)

Easter Term   RK enters the Lower Fourth.

Summer   RK goes to Southsea to bring Trix away from Mrs Holloway. At her house he meets Violet ('Flo') Garrard, whose parents are overseas. She is one or two years older than RK. He falls in love with her, and imagines her to be a Pre-Raphaelite heroine. He asks her to become engaged, and believes that she has agreed to 'an understanding' (as late as September 1882, when he leaves England).

Autumn Term   RK enters the Upper Fourth.

20 December   RK plays Sir Anthony Absolute in Sheridan's *The Rivals*; Dunsterville, Mrs Malaprop; and Beresford, Sir Lucius O'Trigger. Mr H. A. Evans ('Hartopp' in *Stalky & Co.*), the organiser of the natural history society, is also an active promoter of theatricals. Uncle Crom trains RK in précis-writing, an invaluable discipline for the later career of journalism.

1881

Uncle Crom appoints RK as editor of the newly revived *United Services College Chronicle*. (An earlier version folded after three issues.) RK will produce seven issues between 30 June 1881 and 24 July 1882. After he ceases to be editor, 14 issues of the *Chronicle* will print RK's contributions.

Summer Term   RK enters the Lower Fifth. About this time he plays briefly with the idea of becoming a doctor. He visits, several times, St Mary's Hospital at Paddington. (He will claim later that a post-mortem caused him to throw up his immortal soul.) The career of medicine may be momentarily attractive only because he knows that he is unable to attend Oxford or Cambridge. USC lacks the machinery to train candidates for scholarships.

December   Unknown to RK, his mother collects – and his father prints – 23 of his poems under the title *Schoolboy Lyrics*. These are

not collected by RK until he prints 22 of them in *Early Verse*, vol.
XVII of the Outward Bound Edition (1897 and thereafter).

1882

RK publishes his second story, 'Ibbetson Dun', in two instal-
ments in the *Chronicle*, but never completes (or collects) these
fragments.

Easter–Summer Terms RK is in the Upper Fifth. He is awarded
a copy of *Aurora Leigh*, by Elizabeth Barrett Browning, as a parting
gift.

July RK leaves USC after the Summer term, at the age of 16 1/2;
he spends his last summer holiday partly at Rottingdean with the
Burne-Joneses, who had bought North End House there in 1880.
(Dunsterville is going into the Army, and Beresford will become
a civil engineer.)
    JLK is now in his seventh year at Lahore, capital of the
Punjab. He is Principal of the Mayo School of Art, and Curator
of the Lahore Museum, near the Mall. He earns about 1000 rupees
(£90) a month. Lahore, according to the 1875 census, has a population of 92,035 in the city and 36,406 in the suburbs; there are
109,323 Punjabis and 1723 English. The people are predominantly
Muslim. Lahore is an important rail and road junction. The city
has two hospitals, the most important medical school in India, a
training-home for nurses, and a well-staffed prison hospital. The
name of the military cantonment is Mian Mir; here are stationed a
British infantry battalion and a battery of artillery. (RK's favourite
troops will be the Second Battalion of the 5th Northumberland
Fusiliers.) JLK and his wife live in a bungalow on the Mozung
Road. Because it has no vegetation nearby (to discourage snakes
and nuisance animals), the residence is jokingly called by friends
'Bikaner House', after the Great Indian Desert.

20 September RK sails from Tilbury, Essex, on the P & O
steamer *Brindisi*, in drizzling rain.

2 October RK arrives at Port Said. (The Suez Canal has been
open since 1869.)

7 October   RK reaches Suez.

18 October   RK arrives at Bombay. From there he travels the 1000 miles to Lahore by train.

November   RK begins work at the monthly salary of 100 rupees (about £6 13s. 4d.) in the two wooden sheds of the printing-office of the *Civil and Military Gazette*. This newspaper is owned by William Rattigan, a successful lawyer with a social wife; George Allen, who founded the newspaper; and James Walker, a banker and transport business man. His editor is Stephen Wheeler, who had met RK during the Easter holidays, 1882, and – in response to JLK's initiative – thought his talents worthy of a job offer. (Uncle Crom informed RK of the offer.) Within a few weeks after RK's arrival in Lahore, Wheeler is involved in a carriage accident, and confined to bed during Christmas week. RK, not yet 17, has to take charge of 170 workers; though his official title is assistant editor, he and Wheeler are the only white men on the staff. The *Gazette* has only a provincial circulation; it is a subsidiary of the *Pioneer* of Allahabad, a national newspaper, which is owned by Sir George Allen (he likes to publish reports by JLK and AMK); later, proprietors will include Rivett Carnac, Assistant to the Commissioner of the Central Provinces (in 1891 he will become an aide-de-camp to the Queen); Walter Roper-Lawrence, soon to become a secretary to the Viceroy; Edward Buck, Secretary to the government in India; and David Mason, a partner in the newspaper syndicate. RK's office hours are supposed to be 10 a.m. to 4.15 p.m., but he never works less than 10 hours, and often as many as 15. 70 white residents form the Punjab Club, to which RK belongs. He has his own personal servant, Kadir Baksh (the son of JLK's bearer, Mauz Baksh), who shaves him in bed; his *sais*, or groom; and a 'dog boy' who looks after his fox terrier, Vixen.

8 November   'Two Lives', a sonnet, is printed in *The World*. RK receives payment of 1 guinea and is much thrilled by his 'first publication' in the general press.

In this year RK writes 32 poems, binds them, and dates them 1882. The style is *fin de siècle*. The collection is titled *Sundry Phansies*, and eight of the poems will be printed in later volumes.

The book is dedicated to Flo Garrard: 'What have I more to give thee . . . . '

1883

February Because RK knows French, Wheeler assigns him to make abstracts and reports of French-language Russian newspapers, concentrating on items dealing with Afghanistan and the Frontier. The *Gazette* supports the Ilbert Bill, which implements the decision of the Liberal Government in Britain to allow Indian judges to try white people in the courts. RK personally dislikes the Bill, and will later claim (unfairly) that the proprietors wanted honours. He is hissed in the Punjab Club, much to his dismay.

Summer His first hot-weather spell of what will prove to be a lonely year. He is invited to Simla, to stay at the home of James Walker, his employer. Here, in the summer capital of India, RK spends 30 days. (In 1827 the Governor-General spent a summer in Simla; thereafter it became the unofficial residence of the Government during the summer months.)

Late July AMK leaves for England.

August RK returns to Lahore, and his health, attacked by fever and dysentery, fails. JLK remains in Simla.

Autumn JLK goes down to Bengal to prepare a display for the Calcutta Exhibition.

23 December In Lahore, RK plays Desmarets, a police officer, in an amateur theatrical performance of *Plot and Passion*, by Tom Taylor and John Lang. He enjoys his horse, a bay pony named Joe, though the animal is temperamental and hard to manage.

1884

1 January AMK returns to India, and brings Trix with her.
Also this month, RK makes his first public speech at the

Punjab Club on the occasion of a dinner given to the retiring Secretary, who is going to be married.

February He writes to Aunt Edith that he has received his first offer of a bribe from Kizil Bash, in Urdu. (He is one of several Afghan Sirdars who fought against the British in the recent war, and is being kept as a prisoner in Lahore. He wants RK to write stories in the *Gazette* about how 'cruel and unjust' it is to keep him there.) The price offered is 16,000 rupees, about £1300. RK throws back the notes at him, says that he is not a Bunnochi or a Baluchi ('two races the most covetous on earth'), but an English Sahib. He is then offered a Kashmiri girl; finally, his pick of three out of seven horses. He refuses all bribes. (The story has probably been heightened for dramatic purposes.)

March RK goes to Patiala, NW of Simla, to report the state visit of the Viceroy, Lord Ripon, who opens Mohindar College there.

April RK wins the role of Chrysal in the Lahore Amateurs' production of William Schwenk Gilbert's *The Palace of Truth*, but he falls ill after the dress rehearsal, and he never plays the part in public. The play is produced in June.

May JLK, AMK and Trix move to the Hills, leaving RK in Lahore.

July Flo Garrard writes to break off their understanding (in RK's mind, an engagement).
    RK reports on the municipal elections in Lahore.

Summer Cholera epidemic in Lahore; four of the 70 members of the Punjab Club die.

August RK reads *Treasure Island*.

September RK publishes 'The Tragedy of Crusoe, CS', his first lengthy piece of imaginative prose written in India.

29 September The *Gazette* prints 'The Story of Tommy: A Story without a Moral', which some critics regard as the first of RK's barrack-room ballads.

October RK visits Amritsar, site of the Sikhs' Golden Temple. He attends the Great Fair; watches horse-trading, several horse and cattle shows, the awarding of prizes, sports competitions and fireworks.

November *'Echoes' by Two Writers* (RK and Trix) is issued at Lahore. RK will print 32 of these poems as his own in *Early Verse* (1900), but Mrs Fleming will claim that he has taken some of hers (perhaps four).

Toward the end of the year Lord Dufferin arrives as the new Viceroy.

1885

In this year E. Kay Robinson leaves Fleet Street to work for the *Pioneer* in Allahabad.

5 January RK writes a parody of Walt Whitman.

February RK explores the filthy cow-byres of Lahore and Anarkali, a suburb to the south of Lahore.

March RK suffers renewed bouts of 'Lahore sores'.

Late March RK, on an important assignment, visits Rawalpindi and the North-West Frontier (the only time in his life) to cover the Viceroy's reception for Abdur Rahman, the Amir of Afghanistan. (The site of the meeting has been changed to Rawalpindi, which is 180 miles from Lahore, because a Russian regiment threatens the Amir's territory.) RK walks over the frontier to the mouth of the Pass at Jumrood; a hidden tribesman, perhaps a Pathan, fires at him. (There are no wars on the frontier during RK's years in India.)

6 April RK reports on a troop review, which will later be fictionalised in 'Servants of the Queen' in *The Jungle Book*.

30 April–10 May RK leaves on a holiday trip from Simla with De Brath, a friend in the Public Works Department, and his new bride. Unfortunately, he feels out of place as company for the honeymooning couple, and turns back. (Some of his impressions of this trip turn up in 'The Miracle of Purun Bhagat' and *Kim*.)

Summer RK is sent on assignment to Simla for six months to cover the social season. He becomes a regular visitor at the Sunday luncheons of Herbrand Russell, later Duke of Bedford, and meets 'the wittiest woman in India', Mrs Burton, to whom he will dedicate *Plain Tales from the Hills*, his collection of 'turn-overs' (see 1887, 1888).

On 18 July RK attends, at the United Service Institute, a lecture by Major King-Harman on British officers and their weapons.

The Viceroy, Lord Dufferin, often invites the Kiplings to social functions. After his son (Lord Clandeboye) falls in love with Trix and begs her to marry him, Lord Dufferin sends him home to England.

Autumn RK joins B Company of the 1st Punjab Volunteers as a private. His commander asks for his capitation grant, or enrolment fee. RK pays it immediately.

AMK leaves for England during the monsoon season. RK shows Trix his manuscript of *Mother Maturin*, a novel on which he is working. 'Trixie says its [*sic*] awfully horrid; Mother says its nasty but powerful and I know it to be in large measure true. It is an unfailing delight to me . . . . '

December *Quartette*, the Christmas annual of the *Civil and Military Gazette*, is published. The authors are RK, JLK, AMK and Trix. This magazine contains, among other contributions, 'The Strange Ride of Morrowbie Jukes' and 'The Phantom 'Rickshaw'. The authors identify themselves as 'Four Anglo-Indian Writers'. The covers are attributed to the Mayo School of Art in Lahore, which JLK supervises.

1886

RK publishes the first book made entirely of his own work, *Departmental Ditties and Other Verses*. It is printed by the *Gazette* press at Lahore, under his supervision. Its appearance is that of an envelope with flap (resembling an official government file), tied with red tape (actually pink). It is addressed 'To All Heads of Depa...... and all Anglo-Indians'. The first edition consists of 26 poems; the second, 31 poems. Thacker, Spink and Co., Calcutta, is the publisher of the second edition. Several English and Indian editions follow within a year. The third has 41 poems, and the fourth 50 poems. He has written some 350 foolscap pages of *Mother Maturin*, and keeps the manuscript at the bottom of a 'bruised tin tea box'.

January RK inspects an armoured train and writes up an elaborately technical description. (A briefer version of this report will be incorporated in 'The Courting of Dinah Shadd'.)

30 March RK attends the Chiragan Festival, a festival of lamps, held in honour of the Muslim Saint 'Abd al-Qadir Jilani.

5 April RK is admitted as a Freemason to the Lodge Hope and Perseverance, no. 782, EC, at Lahore, by unanimous ballot. He is eight months short of the minimum age of 21. He will serve as the Secretary of the Lodge for three years.

14 April RK watches a demonstration of horse-training, conducted by Captain Matthew Horace Hayes.

15 April He reviews for the *Gazette* Hobson-Jobson's *A Glossary of Colloquial Anglo-Indian Words and Phrases, and of Kindred Terms, Etymological, Historical, Geographical and Discursive*, a London publication (John Murray, 1886), by Sir Henry Yule and Arthur Burnell. He describes it as 'a fascinating volume', 'a glorified *olla podrida* of fact, fancy, note, sub-note, reference, cross-reference, and quotations innumerable, bearing on all things connected directly or indirectly with the East'.

3 May RK passes to the second degree (Freemasons).

Summer RK begins a lifelong friendship with Lord Roberts (Frederick Sleigh Roberts, later Earl Roberts), the well-liked Commander-in-Chief, who holds court at his official residence, called Snowdon.

3 July RK leaves Lahore on a month's leave.

24 August   RK reviews, with distaste, Pratap Chandra Ray's English translation of the *Mahabharata*. He is so annoyed that William Morris has called this one of his '100 Best Books' that he writes a letter expressing his disgust to Uncle Crom. As for the *Ramayana*, 'It is necessary first to peruse an infinity of trivialities before we arrive at anything which may fairly be held to represent oriental *thought*. The rest is dream piled on dream and phantasm on phantasm – unprofitable, and to the Western mind, at least, foolish.'

Autumn   He reads and is greatly impressed by Walter Besant's novel *All in a Garden Fair* (1883). He is becoming convinced that he must seek to establish his literary fortune in London. Sir Ian Hamilton, of the Gordons, sends the manuscript of 'The Mark of the Beast' to England, to be shown to Andrew Lang and William Sharp, and to the editors of two magazines, in an effort to launch RK's career in London. Lang's response: 'I would gladly give Ian a fiver if he had never been the means of my reading this poisonous stuff which has left an extremely disagreeable impression on my mind.' Sharp's response: 'I would strongly recommend you instantly to burn this detestable piece of work. I would like to hazard a guess that the writer of the article in question is very young, and that he will die mad before he has reached the age of thirty.' The story is sent back to India. However, it will be published in *Lloyd's News* in 1890.

October   Andrew Lang describes *Departmental Ditties* in 'At the Sign of the Ship', *Longman's Magazine*. He calls it an anonymous publication (the first edition was printed without any author's name). This review is the first of any work by RK to be published in England.

6 December   RK is raised to Master Mason, Sublime Degree, at the Masonic Hall, Anarkali, Lahore.

In this year RK develops a friendship with a Pathan named Mahbub Ali, who will become an important character in *Kim*.

1887

In this year Stephen Wheeler retires from the *Civil and Military Gazette*. E. Kay Robinson replaces him. Robinson encourages RK to write stories as well as articles (something Wheeler never did). These 'turn-overs', which begin on page 1 and continue on the next page, become a major outlet for RK's creative energies. Robinson's interest in the turn-over derives from his work on the *London Globe*, an evening paper.

10 January RK, who has been serving as Acting Secretary at the Lodge, is unanimously elected Secretary at a regular meeting. RK serves as Charity Steward as well, and collects donations and contributions from Brethren of the Lodge.

18 February RK reports on the early celebration of the Official Jubilee of Queen Victoria, scheduled for 21 June; the date has been advanced four months to avoid India's hot weather.

2 March RK describes the Kaisarin-i-Hind (Empress of India) Bridge, which crosses the Sutlej River (one of five forming the Indus), between Ferozepore and Kazur. This structure will be used as the main prototype of the bridge in 'The Bridge-Builders'.

4 April RK lectures on 'The Origins of the Craft First Degree' at the Masonic Lodge, Anarkali, Lahore. This is his first public lecture. On this day he is advanced to the Mark Degree in Fidelity Mark Lodge no. 98 at Lahore, and is elevated in Mount Ararat Ark Manners' Lodge.

18 May RK reports on the opening of Chak Nizam Bridge, about 100 miles north-west of Lahore.

13 June RK, basing his opinions on newspaper reports, records his first impressions of aircraft, specifically the 23-minute flight of the dirigible balloon *La France*, on 9 August 1884. (No record exists of any flight RK may have taken as a passenger in a balloon or a plane.)

29 June RK writes a somewhat sour commentary on a public services commission which is hearing testimony about the 'employment and treatment of natives in the administration of India'. RK calls it 'a native side-show for the benefit of Anjuman-i-Sabahs, Associations, native newspapers, Subordinate Judges Munsiffs, and so on'.

Summer RK spends a month's leave with his family at Simla.
At Lady Roberts's house, *Summer Home for Nursing Sisters in the
Hills* is staged. (H.J. Byron's burlesque operetta, founded on
Donizetti's opera *Lucia di Lammermoor*, serves as a curtain-raiser.)
RK contributes a 96-line prologue, which Trix, dressed as a nurse,
recites.

The New Gaiety Theatre in the Mall opens with *A Scrap of
Paper*, a translation of a farce by Sardou (the original is called *Les
Pattes de monde*). Mrs Burton plays the leading role; RK plays the
role of Brisemouche.

JLK is made a Companion of the Order of Indian Empire, a
reward for his hard work in improving Indian craft and design,
and helping to insure the success of good Indian Craftsmen.

4 July RK reads a paper, 'Some Remarks on Popular Views
of Freemasonry'.

Early August The *Gazette* is published with new type and a
rearranged layout. 'The House of Shadows' is RK's first turn-over
to appear in the remodelled newspaper (on the 4th).

17 August RK writes an article expressing his admiration of
Lewis Carroll's writings.

27 October RK interviews Dr A. O'Meara, Dental Surgeon of
Upper India, about life in Afghanistan under the rule of Amir
Abdur Rahman.

November On the 7th RK resigns as Secretary of his Mother
Lodge, and asks for a Clearance Certificate to enable him to join
Lodge Independence with Philanthropy in Allahabad. He is about
to leave Lahore, and to say farewell to the soldiers he knows best,
the 5th Northumberland Fusiliers, who are stationed at Mian Mir
(1886–8). In general, RK knows the officers better than he does
the enlisted men.

Also this month, RK is asked to edit the magazine supplement
of the *Pioneer* – *The Week's News* – at Allahabad, and he stops
writing turn-overs.

Allahabad is in Hindu territory. While there, RK lives a
bachelor life, first at the Allahabad Club. He acquires a horse
(Pig and Whistle), and retains his Muslim servant, Kadir Baksh.

He meets 'Aleck' Hill, a devoted photographer and a meterorologist; Hill's main work is as a professor of science at Muir College, and he runs the College Observatory. Lord Salisbury's government has appointed him. RK has been introduced to Hill and his wife, Edmonia, an American woman known as 'Ted', by Sir Edward Buck, an important official in the government, and the author of a book on Simla. The Hills' ramshackle bungalow is called Belvedere. Its garden, sadly neglected, will be used as the home of Rikki-tikki-tavi, the mongoose in *The Jungle Book*.

During November, RK leaves Allahabad for a month in the native states of Rajputana (today called Rajasthan). His articles about this trip are published in the *Pioneer* (Dec 1887 to Feb 1888); these become *Letters of Marque* (1891), and will be reprinted as the first volume of *From Sea to Sea* (1899), a collection of travel pieces. RK visits Agra and the Taj Mahal, Jaipur, Amber, Chitor and Udaipur.

1888

The head of the firm in charge of railway bookstalls in India, Émile Moreau, senior partner in A. H. Wheeler and Co., gives RK a contract in which he assumes all risks for a new series to be entitled the Indian Railway Library. RK writes the contents of the first six paper-bound volumes; the covers are designed by JLK. RK is given $1000, plus a royalty of $20 per 1000 copies after the sales of the first 1500, for publication rights. Titles of RK's contributions: *Soldiers Three* (seven soldier tales), *The Story of the Gadsbys* (a short novel, largely dialogue), *In Black and White* (eight stories about Indians), *Under the Deodars* (six stories about whites, two about Mrs Hauksbee), *The Phantom 'Rickshaw* (four long stories, including 'The Strange Ride of Morrowbie Jukes' and 'The Man Who Would Be King') and *Wee Willie Winkie* (four stories about children).

RK, as assistant editor, reports unsympathetically a meeting of the Congress Party in Allahabad, and refers slightingly to a Congress sympathiser, Captain Hearsey, whose angry reaction is to come to the *Pioneer* office with a horse-whip. He grabs RK, but a staff-member throws the Captain through a bamboo blind on the verandah. The Captain goes to jail for the attack. An action is taken against the *Pioneer* for libel, and a cross-action is brought against the Captain. Sir George Allen, manager and part owner, does not want RK to give evidence, and may have advised him to go on leave and see the world. (This is a controversial point. Other evidence suggests that RK's employers did not want him to leave India for London.) RK has annoyed Lord Dufferin by writing the poem 'One Viceroy to Another', as well as Lord Roberts, his hero, by accusing him of favouritism in military appointments. Mrs Hill, seriously ill with meningitis, decides to recuperate in Pennsylvania, at home. It is time for RK to leave India. The *Pioneer* will pay for his travel reports. The *Gazette* will buy articles from London for two years.

Early this year RK visits Benares briefly, then goes on to Calcutta. ('The City of Dreadful Night', with its title borrowed from James Thomson's poem, consists of seven articles on Calcutta, printed in the *Pioneer* in March.) His visit to the Government's opium factory at Ghazipur on the Ganges shocks him because the profits are so enormous: the Indian Government earns daily a sum equal to two and a half years of the Viceroy's salary.

Trix becomes engaged to John Fleming, a soldier seconded from the Queen's Own Borderers to the Survey Department. She breaks off the engagement, but, one year later, marries him (she is 21). Margaret Burne-Jones writes to RK that she will marry John William Mackail, an Oxford don. RK is displeased by Mackail's liberal politics.

January   'A Little Morality', published in the *Pioneer* in January, attacks the usual English education of Indian boys as being too literary and unsuited for their real needs.

Plain Tales from the Hills appears in its first Indian edition. It is dedicated to 'the wittiest woman in India'. Although several biographers have speculated that RK meant his mother, he also sends a presentation copy to a Mrs Burton – wife of Major F.C. Burton of the Bengal Lancers – at Peshawar, asking her to accept the dedication. (There is no recorded reply.) 39 stories had appeared in the *Civil and Military Gazette*, but RK gathers only 29, and adds 11 more. The first English and American editions will appear in 1890.

April   RK returns to Allahabad as the guest of Professor and Mrs Hill.

May–June RK takes over editorship of the *Gazette* in Lahore (Robinson is away). He finds himself bored by 'the old, wearying, godless futile life at a club' (letter to Mrs Hill).

22 June – 15 July His last season in Simla. He spends considerable time at Sir Edward Buck's villa, called the Retreat. Lord Roberts consults him – while they are riding horses up Simla Mall – about what the men in the barracks are really saying.

December Lord Dufferin retires from service in India, and is replaced by the Marquess of Lansdowne.

1889

January RK leaves the Hills' home because Mrs Hill has fallen severely ill. He says goodbye to his parents in Lahore. He leaves behind his manuscript of *Mother Maturin*, started in 1885. The leading character is an old Irishwoman who keeps an opium den in Lahore, and who sends her daughter to be educated in England. This novel will never be finished, but RK will later cannibalise portions of it for *Kim*.

March RK sells his copyrights of the Indian Railway Library volumes to Émile Moreau for £200; of *Plain Tales from the Hills* for £50; and of *Departmental Ditties* for a small sum. With this money and six months' pay – 4200 rupees, or £275 – he is financially able to leave India. The contract is dated 7 March, but was probably signed by RK several weeks earlier.

3 March RK leaves with the Hills on the *SS Madura* of the British India Line, bound from Calcutta to Rangoon. The ship is known as 'Mutton-Mail' because it delivers both commodities to Burma.

14 March At Rangoon he changes to the *SS Africa*. This in turn makes a call at Moulmein.

24 March Arrives at Singapore, changes to the *Nawab*.

1 April At Hong Kong; while there he visits Canton by *SS Ho-nam*, then changes to the P & O steamer *Ancona*.

15 April Lands in Nagasaki. While in Japan, he visits Kobe, Osaka, Kyoto, Yokohama, Nikko and Tokyo.

11 May Leaves Japan on an American ship, the *City of Peking*.

28 May After 17 days at sea, RK arrives in San Francisco. He delivers a judgement that will do his American reputation some harm: he sees 'with great joy that the block-house which guarded the mouth of the "finest harbour in the world, Sir" could be silenced by two gun-boats from Hong Kong with safety, comfort, and despatch'.

Early June From Portland, Oregon, he goes on a fishing-trip up the Clackamas River, and catches a 12 pound salmon. At Tacoma he is impressed by land speculation.

11 June Trix marries Fleming. After a week in Yellowstone Park, RK goes on to Salt Lake City, Omaha and Chicago, before rejoining the Hills in their parents' home at Beaver, Pennsylvania, on the Ohio. He will stay with them for two months, making trips to Washington, DC, Philadelphia and Boston. He loves Lexington and Concord. At Elmira, New York, he makes a special effort to meet Mark Twain. He becomes engaged to Mrs Hill's younger sister Caroline. The engagement is broken off fairly soon, partly because her father – Professor R.T. Taylor is president of a small college – objects to RK's religious creed. Caroline has been concerned lest RK become a convert to Roman Catholicism. RK writes to her to explain his views: 'I believe in the existence of a personal God to whom we are personally responsible for wrongdoing – that it is our duty to follow and our peril to disobey the ten ethical laws laid down for us by Him and His prophets. I disbelieve directly in eternal punishment. . . . On the same grounds I disbelieve in an eternal reward. As regards the mystery of the Trinity and the Doctrine of Redemption, I regard them most reverently but I cannot give them implicit belief.' (Later, in Villiers Street, London, RK, 'his face beginning to work', tells Trix that the affair has ended.) He travels to Buffalo with Mrs Hill's cousin, Edgar Hill, to see Niagara Falls.

September He arrives in New York, and calls on JLK's friend Mr De Forest, who gives him an introduction to Henry Harper, head of Harper and Brothers. Edwin Abbey, a painter, is also helpful in arranging introductions.

10 September Harper dismisses RK: 'Young man, this house is devoted to the production of literature.'

25 September Mrs Hill, who is returning to India by way of Europe, takes Caroline Taylor with her. Edgar Taylor, their cousin, and RK are members of the party who set sail for England on the *SS City of Berlin*.

October They arrive in Liverpool on the 5th. RK goes on to London, where he stays in North End Road for a few days, then moves to Embankment Chambers at the foot of Villiers Street (no. 19), off the Strand. He lives in a flat on the third floor, looking out on Gatti's famous music hall. Windows at one side of the flat provide a view of the Thames. He is only a few doors away from the London office of the *Pioneer*.

Only a few days later, Andrew Lang takes him to the Savile Club. Mowbray Morris, once Art Editor of the *Pioneer* and now Editor of *Macmillan's Magazine*, accepts 'The Ballad of the King's Mercy' and 'The Ballad of East and West'. Stephen Wheeler, now on the staff of *St James's Gazette*, introduces RK to the Editor, Sidney Low. Andrew Lang, a reader for Sampson Low, Marston and Co., advises the taking-over of the six volumes in the Indian Railway Library. RK negotiates his contract directly.

1890

An edition of 7000 copies of *Soldiers Three* is published early this year for the English market. *The Courting of Dinah Shadd and Other Stories* is published; like several of the stories in the Indian Railway Library, it is reprinted in unauthorised form, this time by Harper and Brothers in New York. (RK had offered these stories to the firm the previous year, but had been rejected.)

Back in India Trix publishes her first novel, *The Heart of a Maid*, under the pseudonym 'Beatrice Grange'. The story describes a family and a courtship very much like her own. The publisher, A. H. Wheeler and Co., Allahabad, prints it as no. 8 of the Indian Railway Library. It will be printed in the United States in 1891, but not in England. The author will be identified as 'Beatrice Kipling'. Mrs W. K. Clifford, a successful minor novelist (she is the widow of William Kingdom Clifford, the scientist, and lives at 26 Colvin Road), introduces RK to several important editors and publishers, and brings him to the house of Macmillan. John W. Lovell, at Wolcott's urging, arranges to publish an authorised American edition of all RK's books; Henry James agrees to write an introduction. Walter Besant introduces RK to A.P. Watt and Son, literary agents. They put his financial affairs and contractual arrangements in order. (The Lovell edition is doubly appreciated by RK because he will get good royalty rates at a time when there is no copyright agreement between the United States and Britain.)

RK enjoys a friendship with W.E. Henley, who prints, with enthusiasm, several of RK's poems in the *Scots Observer*, beginning with the issue of 22 February and continuing in several weekly issues through June. These will be called *Barrack-Room Ballads* when collected and published later in the year. Henley and RK share a dislike of Gladstone's Liberalism. RK enjoys the company of Mrs Molesworth, who, like Mrs Clifford, writes children's books.

Spring Wolcott Balestier, an American literary agent living in London and negotiating royalty arrangements between English authors and J.W. Lovell, an American publishing firm, is introduced to RK at the home of Mrs Humphry Ward, a popular novelist. The two men strike up a warm friendship.

25 March *The Times* publishes a leading article about the Calcutta editions of RK's stories, and praises them highly.

May RK pays a visit to the Paris studio of Flo Garrard and her friend Mabel Price (who will serve as a model for the red-haired girl in *The Light that Failed*). The studio is on the Avenue d'Iéna, near the Étoile.

JLK and AMK arrive from India, on home leave until late summer 1891, and take up residence at 101 Earl's Court Road, London.

June Wolcott Balestier's mother and sisters (Carrie and Josephine) come to London.

July RK agrees to write a novel with Wolcott.
RK and JLK visit the United Services College at Westward Ho! during its Summer Term. A half-holiday is declared in RK's honour.

11 July RK meets Josephine Balestier at Wolcott's lodging.

August RK completes a draft of *The Light that Failed*. He is on the verge of a nervous breakdown; he has been overworked for months.

September Harper and Brothers publish several RK stories without his authorisation in Harper's Franklin Square Library, vol. 680.

October *Departmental Ditties, Barrack-Room Ballads and Other Verses* is published, and enjoys enormous success.
Professor Hill dies prematurely in India. RK will write letters to Mrs Hill in Baltimore until her death in 1952. (She will never meet his wife.)
RK comes down with influenza, and overwork nearly causes the long-anticipated breakdown. The doctor orders him to take a sea voyage. He sails to Naples on the P & O steamer *Shannon*, and stays as an invited guest of Lord Dufferin in Sorrento. (The former Viceroy of India is now British Ambassador in Rome.)

4 October RK publishes in the *Athenaeum* a contribution to 'Literary Gossip'. He accuses Harper and Brothers of literary piracy. Several letters follow, including one signed by Walter Besant, William Black and Thomas Hardy; they claim that in their experience Harper and Brothers have always been fair to foreign authors. The Balestier family live on the Isle of Wight, in Wolcott's seaside cottage.

25 October RK's name comes up for election to the Savile. Andrew Lang proposes his acceptance; the nomination is supported by Walter Besant, James Bryce, Edward Clodd, John Collier, Sidney Colvin, Austin Dobson, Edmund Gosse, Rider

Haggard, Thomas Hardy, William Ernest Henley, Henry James, J.H. McCarthy, J.W. Mackail, Walter Pollock, George Saintsbury and others. (His election follows on 30 Jan 1890.) At the Club RK enjoys the company of Lang, Haggard and Anstey (T.A. Guthrie), as well as that of his cousins Ambrose Poynter and Philip Burne-Jones. He dislikes Sidney Colvin, George Meredith and 'long-haired literati'.

7 November J.B. Lippincott publishes a 12-chapter version of *The Light that Failed* in London as a copyright issue, and it is printed in *Lippincott's Monthly Magazine*, January 1891. RK receives $800 as payment (according to McClure's *Autobiography*). As a consequence of its curious publishing history, two versions of the novel will circulate: one with 14 chapters, has a sad ending, and the other, with 12 chapters, a happy one. It is unclear whether AMK urged the happy ending on her son; there has also been speculation that Flo Garrard was responsible.

Winter Possibly on 28 November, RK meets Wolcott's elder sister, Caroline (she is three years older than RK) in Wolcott's one-room office at Dean's Yard, behind Westminster Abbey. (In midsummer Wolcott had brought Carrie, her sister Josephine, and her mother over to London to keep house for him.) Wolcott's grandfather, Judge Peshine Smith, is a lawyer with an international reputation; he served as legal adviser to the Emperor of Japan. Beatty (pronounced 'Baty' in Brattleboro, Vermont) is Carrie's brother; he accompanied the family to London, but stayed very briefly; he is so troublesome that he is sent back to the United States in late July (RK does not meet him at this time).

The early courtship of RK and Carrie does not run smoothly. AMK unhappily says, 'That woman is going to marry our Ruddy.' JLK notes that Carrie is 'a good man spoiled'.

Robert Louis Stevenson is so impressed by *Soldiers Three* that he writes a letter of congratulations to RK. An exchange of correspondence follows.

6 December RK publishes a poem, 'The Rhyme of the Three Captains', characterising Besant, Black and Hardy as pirates, and attacking Harper and Brothers.

13 December Harper and Brothers announce that 'The Record of Badalia Herodsfoot' – the serial rights of which have been acquired by purchase – will be substituted for 'The Incarnation of Krishna Mulvaney'. RK is not mollified.

25 December The last reunion of the Kiplings' 'family square'.

1891

RK suppresses *The City of Dreadful Night and Other Sketches*, which A. H. Wheeler and Co. have prepared for publication. *Letters of Marque*, later to become the first volume of *From Sea to Sea*, is also published in India and England. *American Notes*, a series of letters originally sent to the *Pioneer*, is published in New York. *Mine Own People* is printed with a defensive letter by RK, protesting that he is trying to prevent unauthorised publication of some of its stories in the United States. *Life's Handicap*, also published this year, contains all the stories in *Mine Own People*, together with 16 additional stories and one poem.

JLK publishes *Beast and Man in India*, to which RK contributes two poems, verse headings for nine of the chapters, and extracts from two letters.

W. E. Henley prints RK's 'The English Flag' as the first poem in his new anthology, *Lyra Heroica* ('And what they should know of England who only England know?').

March *The Light that Failed* is published in a 14-chapter version.

May–June RK makes a short visit to the United States with his uncle Fred Macdonald, a minister. They intend to see RK's eldest uncle, Harry, who is in New York and is ailing. RK crosses the Atlantic on a German ship, under the name of J. Macdonald; but Harry dies while they are in mid-Atlantic. Reporters meet RK at the dock. He hates their inquisitiveness about what he regards as private matters.

July RK quits Embankment Chambers.

Midsummer RK visits Wolcott, his mother, Josephine and Carrie on the Isle of Wight. He is depressed by the 'torpid atmosphere'.

22 August   RK leaves Southampton on the Union Castle steamer *SS Mexican*. J. M. Cook sees him off. The ship stops at Madeira before going on to Cape Town (10 Sep). At Simonstown, at the Cape Naval Station, he visits the admiral in charge. Captain Bayly (whom he has met on the *Mexican*) invites him on a cruise, which will lead to the writing of RK's first naval story, 'Judson and the Empire'.

25 September   RK embarks for New Zealand on the Shaw Savill steamer *SS Doric*; the trip lasts 24 days ending at Wellington on 18 October.

22 October   Beginning today, RK travels to Auckland. He takes a train to Napier, then proceeds by buggy to Taupo, and on, past the gorges in the Runanga bush and across the Maungaharuru mountain range, to the Kaingaroa Plains. From there he continues to Wairakei and its hotel, called 'Mr Robert Graham's Establishment'; on by way of the Ateamuri road to Rotorua and Cambridge (a farming district of the Waikato); and by train to Auckland.

26 October   A dramatised version of *The Naulahka* is given a copyright performance (i.e. a reading) at the Opera Comique, London. Henry James and Edmund Gosse are present.

29 October   RK leaves Auckland (where he may have met Sir George Grey) for New Plymouth, sailing on the 423-ton *Mahinapua*; from there he proceeds by train back to Wellington.

2 November   On the Union steamship *SS Talune* RK crosses the Tasman Sea to Port Lyttleton.

3 November   RK visits Christchurch and renews acquaintance with F. W. Haslam, a former Latin master at the United Services College, and now a professor.

4 November   Port Chalmers, with a visit to Dunedin, and Bluff.

6 November   RK embarks on the *Talune* for a three-week visit to Australia.

14 November   At Sydney RK takes the *SS Valetta*, which is scheduled to call at the ports of Melbourne and Adelaide. By now the tightness of his schedule has made impossible a trip to Samoa, to visit Robert Louis Stevenson. (RK, invited by the *Melbourne Age* to report on the race for the Melbourne Cup – run on 3 November – and flattered by this 'most distinguished honour', cites as his reason for not doing so the fact that he knows it is not in his line. Also, he would have had to rearrange the dates of his itinerary.) He enjoys sightseeing in Melbourne.

From Adelaide RK continues on the *Valetta* to Colombo, Ceylon, arriving in early December. His fellow traveller is General Booth of the Salvation Army. It is possible that he learns of Wolcott Balestier's fatal illness for the first time in Colombo, though more likely that the news is brought to him when he arrives home in Lahore. From Colombo he takes the SS *Narbudda* to Tuticorin, on the south coast of India. From there he travels by train for four days and nights to Lahore, arriving a few days before Christmas. This is Kipling's only encounter with southern India.

At approximately the same time Wolcott is trying, in partnership with Heinemann, to publish English and American works on the continent of Europe; the model is Tauchnitz ('The English Library').

6 December Wolcott dies suddenly of typhoid in Dresden (his illness had first manifested itself in England). His mother and two sisters join him before the end. RK learns, from a cable sent to him from London, that Wolcott has died. He leaves immediately (before Christmas Day) for Bombay.

27 December After a brief visit to his old ayah, RK leaves India for England.

Around this time, Henry James comes to help the Balestiers. Carrie sells the Balestier home on the Isle of Wight.

1892

10 January RK arrives at Victoria Station, London, and is greeted by Mrs Balestier and daughters.

18 January RK marries Carrie Balestier at All Souls' Church, Langham Place, London. The only relative present is Ambrose Poynter, who stands for RK; Henry James stands for Carrie (whom he does not like). Also present are William Heinemann, Philip and Tessa Gosse, and Edmund Gosse. RK attends a wedding-breakfast with Ambo Poynter at Brown's Hotel, and there signs his will on a piece of hotel notepaper.

26 January   When he is preparing to leave Brown's, the manager, Henry Ford, presents him with a receipted bill for £22. For the next 43 years RK will stay at Brown's on most occasions when he visits London; he will always reserve the same suite. RK moves with Carrie to 101 Earl's Court Road.

2 February   The Kiplings leave London for Liverpool. RK has bought two Cook's tickets for a round-the-world voyage ('The Long Trail'). Henry James comes to see them off, accompanied by William Heinemann and Bram Stoker.

3 February   The Kiplings sail from Liverpool for New York on the *SS Teutonic*. Henry Adams is a fellow-passenger.

Mid-February   They arrive in Brattleboro, Vermont ('Thirty below freezing!'). The Kiplings step from the train and enter a waiting sleigh piled high with blankets and buffalo robes. Beatty Balestier drives them to Maplewood, his own home, where he lives with his wife, Mai Mendon Balestier.

20 February   Beginning today, RK visits New York, Chicago, St Paul, Winnipeg, and the Rocky Mountains, in order to write travel sketches for the *Civil and Military Gazette*, the *New York Sun* and *The Times* (London).

March   RK buys the ground on which his home Naulakha will be built, according to the land records of the town of Dummerston.

Late March   RK buys 20 acres of land in north Vancouver, and will pay taxes for years before discovering that it belongs to somebody else, and never legally has been his property.

April   *The Naulahka: A Story of East and West*, a collaboration with Wolcott, who wrote the opening chapters about the American West, is published. RK contributes the chapters about India. (Wolcott is probably responsible for the misspelling of the title.)

Also this month, *Barrack-Room Ballads and Other Verses* is published in both Britain and the United States. The book will be reprinted three times this year, 50 times over the next decade.

4 April The Kiplings leave on the *Empress of India* for Japan.

20 April The ship reaches Yokohama Bay.

May An earthquake hits Yokohama.

9 June RK withdraws a small sum of money from the Yokohama branch of his bank, the New Oriental Banking Corporation, with its head office at 40 Threadneedle Street, London. The manager urges him to withdraw more, but RK refuses. That afternoon he learns that the bank has failed, and that he has lost nearly £2000. In his desperation he forms a 'Committee of Ways and Means' to give all depositors a voice; he moves that creditors should accept 25 per cent of their deposit in deferred shares, and give the bank one year to pay. He cashes in his unexpended vouchers at Cook's. This financial disaster ends RK's intention of visiting Robert Louis Stevenson in Vailima.

27 June The Kiplings leave on the *Empress of China* for Vancouver. On arrival, the Canadian Pacific Railway takes them back across Canada free of charge, courtesy of William Van Horne, Chairman of the Railway.

9 August The Kiplings arrive in Brattleboro.

Late summer While Naulakha is being built, they live in Bliss Cottage, named after the original owners, and pay a rent of £2 a month to Carrie's mother, who holds the lease. This cottage is usually the house of a hired man. RK acquires from Beatty a pasture of 11 1/2 acres.

Autumn RK outlines 'Mowgli's Brothers', inspired partly by a scene in H. Rider Haggard's *Nada the Lily*.

Winter Carrie takes over the household accounts. RK is becoming much more conscious of the pride of Mme Balestier, Carrie's mother, who lives in Beechwood, a Colonial-style house built in 1868. She comes from a large and well-known family, the members of which have included three governors of Connecticut and one signatory of the Declaration of Independence. Joseph Balestier, Carrie and Beatty's grandfather, died in 1888, leaving behind a considerable fortune of more than $600,000.

29 December   The Kiplings have a daughter, whom they name after Carrie's sister Josephine.

1893

During this year RK builds his house, called Naulakha, near Mount Monadnock. ('Naulakha' means 9 lakhs of rupees, and a lakh is worth 100,000 rupees.) Jean Pigeon, from Quebec, does the work; Henry Rutgers Marshall is the architect. The house rests on a high foundation of solid rocks. The roof and sides are covered by dull-green, hand-split shingles. JLK visits the construction site before the house is finished, and contributes a motto, taken from St John, 'The night cometh when no man can work'; this is modelled in plaster for the mantelpiece above the fireplace.

June   *Many Inventions*, a collection of 14 stories and two poems, is published.

Summer   The Kiplings move into Naulakha. RK develops friendships with Mary Cabot, a close acquaintance of Wolcott; Mrs Holbrook and the aged former governor of Vermont (during the Civil War); Charles Eliot Norton of Harvard; and Dr James Conland, who attended Carrie when she gave birth to Josephine. Matthew Howard, the groom, takes them for drives, and on one notable occasion saves Carrie from a carriage accident.

End of November   RK's income for the year is £3000.
    JLK, who retired in May of this year, receives his pension. In Lahore the school and museum called the Victoria Jubilee Institute – which JLK designed largely by himself – is completed. It will be called in later years the Mayo School of Art, like the earlier group of artists working under JLK's direction.

Winter RK learns how to ski, and how to walk on snowshoes. He paints his golf-balls red so that he will not lose them in the snow.

1894

The Jungle Book, consisting of seven stories and seven poems, is published.

March RK sails to Bermuda, and meets a family from New Jersey, Mrs Julia Catlin and her two daughters. He enjoys a meal at the sergeants' mess.

April The Kiplings visit England. RK's parents are living at Tisbury, in the Wiltshire Downs; their house is called the Gables. The RKs live in Tisbury for six months, in Arundell House. The location proves to be too far from both London and the sea.

May RK attends a dinner at which he sits between Mr Astor and Lord Roberts. He proposes a toast to Lord Roberts and to the British Army.

May or June In London he meets Aubrey Beardsley.

25 July He revisits Westward Ho! Cormell Price retires; RK contributes £20, and makes a speech on behalf of the 'Old Boys'. Uncle Crom will live 15 years in retirement. In London RK buys back from Wheeler the British copyright of the first six Indian Railway Library books. The price is £1200. Wheeler retains the Indian sales for himself.

5 August The Kiplings sail for the United States.

28–9 November Arthur Conan Doyle pays a visit, and plays golf with RK (not the first time for RK, who enjoyed the sport with his neighbours the Cabots). RK reads 'McAndrew's Hymn' to Doyle, who is much impressed. They eat Thanksgiving dinner at Maplewood, Beatty Balestier's home.

December RK tallies his earnings for the year: £5000. He works on the life-story of Kim O'rishti, but abandons it in favour of *Captains Courageous*. Word of Robert Louis Stevenson's death reaches RK on the 3rd, and he becomes so upset that he does not write anything for a week.

1895

The Second Jungle Book, consisting of eight stories and eight poems, plus two verse headings, is published.

January Carrie is severely burned by shooting flames at the furnace door. After a fortnight of illness, she recovers; but her brown hair has turned grey. She travels to Washington, DC, for a protracted recovery of six weeks. RK meets, and likes, Theodore Roosevelt, head of the Civil Service Commission. He visits Congress in the company of Cecil Spring Rice. The ways of national legislators make a very disagreeable impression on him. He meets John Hay at the State Department, and Professor S.P. Langley of the Smithsonian Institution. He is invited to the White House to meet President Grover Cleveland. He becomes disgusted by 'a colossal agglomeration of reeking bounders' in the White House. He also makes the acquaintance of Bliss Carman, a 'so-called' poet.

March RK completes 'The Spring Running', the last of his Mowgli stories.

Summer The United States argues with Great Britain over the Venezuela–British Guiana frontier. The president becomes unusually aggressive. RK expects war, and makes preparations for his family to escape into Canada; he also makes sure that they will not starve if open hostilities break out. He replaces Rod and Ric, his undependable carriage-horses, with a new pair of thoroughbreds.

June RK establishes his own personal post office. Hallett Phillips, a Washington lawyer who loves American wildlife, arranges it with President Cleveland's help. The post office is named Waite after the postmistress, Anna F. Waite.

6–14 July The Kiplings, taking their usual summer tour, cross the Atlantic in a German ship, the *Saale*.

July   The Kiplings visit JLK at Tisbury, and RK calls on the 'dear old ladies' of Warwick Gardens, near Kensington High Street.

Autumn   RK is nominated by Lockwood de Forest, and seconded by Richard Watson Gilder, for the Century Club, New York City. He is admitted, and remains a member for the rest of his life.

Winter   Frank N. Doubleday brings RK an offer from Scribner's to publish a complete edition of RK's works. RK will call him FND, or 'Effendi', for the rest of his life.

Christmas   Carrie's mother comes to Naulakha and stays for several days.

1896

Tensions between RKs and Beatty erupt in this year. Wolcott had charged Carrie to take care of Beatty, and RK believed that he had to share this responsibility with his wife. In 1893 Beatty was given the task of superintending the workmen doing the outdoor work on Naulakha. But he frequently quarrelled with Matt Howard, and matters were not improved when Carrie accused her brother of appropriating money he had been given to pay the workmen. Beatty, for his part, claimed that she was trying to drive him into bankruptcy. An especially strong quarrel blew up over the cost of the walkway in front of Naulakha. Moreover, every time Beatty came to visit the Kiplings, he was (or seemed to be) drunk.

2 February   A second daughter, Elsie, is born.

March   The *New York Sunday World* offers RK a dollar a word for 1000 words on the subject 'America can never conquer England'. RK refuses the offer. He travels with Dr Conland to Gloucester, Massachusetts, and T Wharf in Boston Harbour to carry on the research needed for authentication of various scenes in his new novel, *Captains Courageous: A Story of the Grand Banks*. In this month Beatty petitions for bankruptcy.

April The Kiplings visit New York, and stay at 262 Fourth Avenue. RK meets Stephen Crane. He takes lessons in a New York school to learn how to ride a bicycle.

6 May RK, on his way to Waite's Corner to pick up mail, is almost struck down in the pines by Beatty's team of horses, which are being driven carelessly. RK falls off his bicycle. Beatty, in a rage, demands that RK retract lies that he claims have been circulated about himself, and threatens RK with personal violence.

9 May The Kiplings send a sheriff to arrest Beatty for assault. A preliminary hearing takes place in the office of Judge William S. Newton, who holds Beatty pending a hearing. RK offers to supply bail for Beatty, but Beatty refuses to accept the tentative gesture of goodwill.

12 May A hearing in the Town Hall. So many reporters from Boston, New York, Philadelphia and Washington attend that the hearing is transferred to a larger assembly hall, one in which the town meetings take place. C.C. Fitts, State Attorney, is the prosecutor. Haskins, an attorney, is appointed for RK. George Hill represents Beatty. The case is put off for the September term of court. Beatty is ordered to give bail of $400 to keep the peace, and another $400 for his appearance at County Court. RK is deeply upset by the proceedings.

Late May RK spends a fortnight with Lockwood de Forest on the Gaspé Coast; he enjoys salmon-fishing.

29 August RK leaves the United States on the *SS Lahn*. He will return only once, in 1899.

9 September The Kiplings arrive in Southampton.
    Soon afterwards, RK rents Rock House in Maidencombe, a village near Torquay, Devon. He describes it as 'a big stone and stucco Naulakha, long, low with two stories, stuck on the side of a steep hill'. RK's more unfavourable judgement of it may be found in 'The House Surgeon'. The house, writes RK after abandoning it (the winter of 1896–7 is particularly wet, cold and unpleasant) is 'a lovely place but eight months damp,

rain, sea fog and mildew were rather more than we would stand'.

Autumn RK and Carrie cycle on a tandem machine with double handlebars. Each believes that the other enjoys it. Neither does.

3 October William Morris dies.

October RK visits the officers of the old three-decker *Britannia* at Dartmouth. He meets again Captain E.H. Bayly, RN, whom he had known at Cape Town in 1891. He is invited to go aboard 'a new 20-knot cruiser', for naval manoeuvres. RK finds this more exhilarating than the possibility of serving as a war correspondent based on Crete, reporting on the clash between the Turks and Cretans. Ambo and Hugh Poynter visit the Kiplings at Rock House; so does JLK, who sets up a studio in the coach-house. RK finishes his book of *Verses, 1889–1896*, and arranges his stories by groups for the Outward Bound Edition, published by Charles Scribner's, New York. JLK makes pictures for the edition. Frank Doubleday, soon to set up his own publishing-house, plans to publish all American editions of RK's works from now on. Uncle Crom also pays a visit. RK finishes *Captains Courageous*, and sells the serial rights for $10,000 to *McClure's Magazine*.

13 December RK begins work on *Stalky & Co.*, and within six weeks reads to his cousin Florence Macdonald the drafts of some stories destined for inclusion in this work.

1897

2 April RK is elected to the Athenaeum as a person eminent in public life. Not yet 32, he is the youngest member. On the day of his admission, he dines with Alfred Milner, Cecil Rhodes and the Editor of *The Times*. Sir Walter Besant and Sir Sidney Colvin, members of the General Committee, nominated him, and Henry James seconded the nomination.

17 April A new painting by Philip Burne-Jones, of a vampire-like woman, inspires RK to write a poem ('a rag and a bone and a hank of hair'); published in the *Daily Mail*, the poem creates a sensation. The painting is exhibited at the New Gallery a week later.

11 May   Carrie is expecting another child. The Kiplings leave Torquay, and move to the Royal Palace Hotel, Kensington.

May   RK attends the Royal Academy banquet, sits next to Sir Henry Irving and Alfred Austin, the Poet Laureate. Sir John Thorneycroft, the sculptor, invites him to attend the steam-trials of a new 30-knot destroyer which sails from Chatham on the Medway to the Thames, and from the Mouse Light to the Lower Hope reach on the Thames. Sir William Wilson-Hunter, a distinguished retired Indian administrator and an historian of India, invites RK to be his guest at Oaken Holt, near Oxford. He takes him to dine at High Table at Balliol. The undergraduates give RK a standing ovation. A special Bach concert in his honour follows.

RK goes to the Lyceum. Sir Henry Irving puts a private box at his disposal, and asks RK to write a play for him. RK goes backstage to visit both Irving and Miss Ellen Terry.

2 June   The Kiplings go to Brighton to avoid the Diamond Jubilee celebration in London. They stay at North End House, Rottingdean, 4 miles from Brighton, for the summer. This is the summer home of the Burne-Joneses, and William Morris has furnished it. During this summer RK forms close ties with Stanley Baldwin. The Ridsdales live in the Dene, on one side of the village green. RK decides to rent the Elms, also on the green, and 100 feet from North End House.

11 June   RK attends a luncheon for the colonial premiers in London, and meets the High Commissioner for Canada.

15 June   At work on 'The White Man's Burden'.

22 June   Writes a poem 'After', a draft of what will become 'Recessional'. Dissatisfied with it, he throws the manuscript into a wastepaper basket. Sallie Norton reclaims it and urges him to publish it. After revisions, RK sends the five-stanza poem – Aunt Georgie acting as messenger – to C.F. Moberly Bell, Manager of *The*

Times, and Bell publishes the poem on 17 July. (This manuscript is today in the British Museum.)

Summer Captain Bayly invites both RK and JLK to Portsmouth to visit *HMS Pelorus*. The Naval Review to mark Queen Victoria's Diamond Jubilee has just concluded. RK witnesses smaller-scale manoeuvres of the Channel Squadron. These are described in *A Fleet in Being*.

17 August John, the Kiplings' third child, is born, and named after JLK. The delivery takes place in North End House.

25 September The Kiplings move to the Elms, which they have been renting for 3 guineas a week. But RK continues house-hunting, and visits Dorchester to try making the rounds with Thomas Hardy. The search is unsuccessful. (One landlady, it turns out, has never heard of either Kipling or Hardy.)

Autumn Visitors at the Elms include 'Uncle Ned' (Sir Edward Burne-Jones), 'Uncle Crom', Sydney Cockerell, J.M. Barrie, Arthur Sullivan (who wants to set 'Recessional' to music), William Ernest Henley and Beerbohm Tree (who wants RK to write a play for him). In October he reads stories from the unfinished *Stalky & Co.* to Cormell Price and Sir Sydney Cockerell. RK develops his first interest in motor cars, specifically a 5-horsepower tube ignition model.

Trix publishes her second novel, *A Pinchbeck Goddess*, about marital bickering and social life in Simla. Heinemann in England, and D. Appleton Co. in New York, publish the book, which has disturbing autobiographical overtones. (It was originally published as a brief sketch in the *Civil and Military Gazette*, 10 Dec 1886, anonymously, as one of 39 stories under the title *Plain Tales from the Hills*, 2 Nov 1886 – 10 June 1887. The novel is an expansion of the sketch.)

JLK decorates a room in Indian style at the house of the Duke of Connaught. Later, he will arrange a suite of Indian rooms at Osborne, at the request of the Queen; he will supervise the work of a Hindu craftsman, Bai Ram Singh.

After lengthy negotiations, RK's agent, A. P. Watt, repurchases from Thacker and Co. the copyright of *Departmental Ditties* for £2000.

1898

An Almanac of Twelve Sports, a set of verses written for William Nicholson's *Almanac of Sports*, is basically a calendar for 1898. Each month shows a block print of an English sport appropriate for the given season, and Kipling's verse is similarly relevant. (Nicholson lives in Rottingdean.) Also in this year RK publishes *The Day's Work*, 12 stories written in Vermont, and published in periodicals. *A Fleet in Being: Notes of Two Trips with the Channel Squadron* is a reprint of articles originally appearing in *The Times* and the *Morning Post*; RK is describing his second summer cruise (1898) on *HMS Pelorus* with the Channel Squadron, as the guest of Captain Bayly, and his visit to Bantry Bay (his first visit to Ireland). RK visits several ships in the squadron.

8 January The Kiplings embark at Southampton for Madeira (which impresses RK) and Cape Town, on the *SS Dunvegan Castle*. JLK accompanies them, and stays with them for three months. On arrival in Cape Town, they go to a boarding-house at Newlands – the Vineyard – on the slope of Table Mountain. Sir Alfred Milner, the Queen's High Commissioner, invites them out several times, as does Cecil Rhodes. Milner has been delegated by Joseph Chamberlain, the Colonial Secretary, to arrange a settlement between the British Empire and the two Boer republics.

25 January Edgar Wallace publishes 'Tommy to his Laureate' in *Cape Times*; this poem, welcoming RK to South Africa, leads to the beginning of a personal friendship. RK meets Wallace at a dinner in Cape Town, and gives him 'encouragement and good advice'. (Wallace's poem is later printed in *Writ in Barracks*.)

March Rhodes sends RK to visit his province of Rhodesia.
    RK travels from Kimberley to 'Khama's country', and then on to 'the great grey-green greasy Limpopo River all setabout with fever-trees'. He explores Bulawayo, and, with Sir Charles Metcalfe, visits the Matoppo Hills. He returns by way of Johannesburg to Cape Town (end of March).

April The Kiplings return to England. The night of their arrival in London, John Hay, the American Minister, visits RK at his hotel, and discusses with him the Spanish–American War.

7 April An abortive production of *The Light that Failed*, a one-act version by Courtney Thorpe, opens at the Royalty.

14 May RK writes 'A Few Hints of Schoolboy Etiquette' for *The School Budget*, published by the Horsmonden School in Kent, which has offered to pay him at the rate of 3d. per page.

16 May RK gives a dinner speech about his impressions of South Africa to members of the Anglo-African Writers Club. Rider Haggard is chairman.

17 June Sir Edward Burne-Jones dies in London. His ashes are buried in the little church at Rottingdean. RK's final tribute: 'He was more to me than any other man.'

Summer He reads the *Just So Stories* to Josephine, Elsie, and John and Angela Mackail, Aunt Georgie's grand-daughter. RK approves a dramatised version of *The Light that Failed*. This will be produced by Sir Johnston Forbes-Robertson, who plays Dick Helder, at the Lyric in February 1903; it will be revived at the Drury Lane on 31 March, 1913.

December Trix's mind gives way, and AMK takes care of her at Tisbury. Trix spends much of the next three years in nursing-homes.

1899

Stalky & Co., nine stories and one poem, dealing with student life at the United Services College, is published in both Britain (6 Oct) and the United States. 'Stalky', a separate story, will be collected in *Land and Sea Tales* (1923). *The Complete Stalky & Co.* (1929) will add another four stories and four poems. Also published in this year: *From Sea to Sea and Other Sketches*, two volumes of letters, sketches and stories written up to (and including) 1890. (The first British edition is printed in 1900.) 'Recessional' is printed in various editions, some unauthorised, and becomes one of the most popular poems of the decade.

January–February The Kiplings sail for the United States on 20 January. Carrie wants to see her mother, and RK wants to settle some publishing-arrangements in New York. The crossing of the Atlantic is stormy and unpleasant. Carrie falls ill. In Vermont, Beatty threatens a lawsuit against RK. A piracy suit against Putnam's occupies RK's energies, but by 20 February he succumbs himself, in the Hotel Grenoble on West 56th Street, New York.

Inflammation spreads from one lung to both; he is suffering from acute lobar pneumonia. The doctors think that he may die. The German Kaiser and Henry James, among countless well-wishers, send telegrams and letters. The children, who have undergone a long, bone-chilling wait in a drafty customs house on entering New York (2 Feb), develop bad colds. Little Josephine's sickness is aggravated by a very high temperature. Carrie sends her to their old family friend, Lockwood de Forest, to see whether her whooping-cough, with complications, can be more easily cured away from the hotel. Doctors in attendance upon RK are Theo Dunham (Carrie's brother-in-law), Edward G. Janeway and James Conland, who has come down from Brattleboro to help. RK's chief nurse is Miss Helen M. Warner. His crisis begins on 28 February.

4 March RK's crisis passes, and his temperature falls. He is no longer in danger.

6 March Josephine dies, at 6.30 a.m. She is seven years old. RK is not informed immediately because of his own medical problem. (See p. 86, entry for Frank Doubleday.)

17 April Frank Doubleday takes RK to a private hotel, the Laurel House, Lakewood, New Jersey.

9 May RK moves to Morristown to stay with Mrs Julia Catlin.

22 May The doctor advises RK to do no work for six months, and to rest for two hours daily.

June Carrie goes one last time to Naulakha to collect some belongings.

JLK comes to the United States. Watt, RK's literary agent,

tries to sort out various copyright quarrels. RK brings a suit in US courts, and loses it.

24 June   The Kiplings, Edward Bok, JLK and the Frank Doubledays sail for England on the *SS Teutonic*. The Kiplings will never visit the United States again. Andrew Carnegie offers them the use of a small house in the Scottish Highlands. Carrie accepts.

Summer   Sara Anderson, the former secretary of John Ruskin, George Meredith and George Moore, comes to work as RK's private secretary.

July   Philip Burne-Jones paints RK's portrait (now in the National Portrait Gallery). RK, delighted, calls it 'a Regular Stunner'. He works with the artist on a hand printing-press at the Elms.

August   The Kiplings take up Carnegie's offer. The house is located on the American millionaire's estate in Sutherland. The RKs visit Dunrobin Castle (JLK accompanies them). They travel on Carnegie's steam yacht.

Autumn   RK is exhilarated by his first experiments with a motor car. He is impressed by the fact that Harmsworth of the *Daily Mail* can visit him easily in a motor car, and in December he will hire a motor from Brighton, capable of 8 miles an hour and complete with an 'engineer', at $3^1/_2$ guineas a week.

October   Outbreak of the Boer War. RK forms a volunteer company (30–40 members) in Rottingdean. He serves as chairman of its managing committee. The men practise on a 1000-yard rifle-range at the Lustrals on the Downs; they are drilled by petty officers of the coastguards. RK gives the club a Nordenfelt machine-gun that he has brought back from South Africa.

17 October   Henry James lunches with the Kiplings.

31 October   RK publishes 'The Absent-Minded Beggar' in the *Daily Mail*. It rapidly becomes the biggest money-earning poem of RK's career, and nets more than £250,000. The money goes to a fund designed to help the wives and children of soldiers who are fighting in South Africa. The poem is printed on cotton handkerchiefs, and on silk for benefit programmes; and is set to music by Sir Arthur Sullivan.

14 December   R. Macdonald, Lord Salisbury's secretary, offers RK a Knighthood (it is proposed to make him a Knight Commander of the Bath). Although pleased by the honour, RK declines, feeling that he 'can do better without it'.

1900

20 January   The RKs leave England on the *RMS Kinfauns Castle* for South Africa.

5 February   They reach Cape Town.

6 February   Lord Roberts gives RK a pass to go anywhere in South Africa. During his stay RK befriends several journalists, including Leopold Stennett Amery of *The Times*; H.A. Gwynne of Reuter's; and Perceval Landon, also of *The Times*. He confers with Lord Roberts before the latter goes on to take command of the Army in the field. The centre of activity in Cape Town is the Mount Nelson Hotel, on the slope of Table Mountain. (It is nicknamed the 'Helot's Rest' by a statesman.) RK visits various military hospitals. He travels with Cecil Rhodes to the Western Province. Rhodes decides to build a house on the Groote Schuur estate for artists and men of letters. He offers it to the Kiplings, who will become the first tenants.

29 February   Paardeberg, an important battle, is fought. RK goes in an ambulance train to the rail-head at Modder River, and returns with a trainload of wounded.

7 March   Carrie works with an architect, Herbert Baker (who will become a lifelong friend) to help select a site for the house that Rhodes has commissioned. It will be built in the Dutch Colonial style.

17 March   RK joins the staff of *The Friend of the Free State*, a newspaper in Bloemfontein, capital of the Orange Free State. Lord Roberts has sponsored it, so it is an official Army publication.

The first issue appeared on 16 March, and it will appear daily until 30 April. RK edits copy for 26 issues, writes stories and corrects proofs. His contributions will later be reprinted in *War's Brighter Side*, edited by Julian Ralph (1901). RK founds a dining-club, 'The Friendlies', and designs a badge and an elaborate Masonic ritual. He nurses Lester, the son of Julian Ralph (a fellow war correspondent, and an American), through a spell of typhoid (enteric fever).

19 March   RK goes to the front, and sees troops under fire at Karee Siding. Here the British suffer 180 casualties.

31 March   Ambush of Sanna's Post; the British lose 155 men.

3 April   RK returns to Cape Town. He enjoys the company of Mary Kingsley (he had met her in West Kensington); she is about to begin work in a fever hospital at Simonstown.

28 April   RK returns to London.

May   He dines with Joseph Chamberlain.

June (and often thereafter)   The Kiplings visit St Loe Strachey, editor of the *Spectator*, and his wife, near Guildford, Surrey.

3 June   Mary Kingsley dies of fever at Simonstown. This illness was caused by overwork in nursing Boer prisoners.

3 July   Carrie writes in her diary that the manuscript of *Mother Maturin* has been sent to RK by his literary agent, A. P. Watt. RK borrows portions of it for *Kim*. (The manuscript has since disappeared.)

Summer   RK hires a 24-horsepower steam-driven American car called a Locomobile. It drives erratically; RK calls it the 'Holy Terror', and renames it the 'Octopod' in 'Steam Tactics'.

August   The Kiplings visit Bateman's, Burwash, Sussex, for the first time. They are pleased with its beauty and relatively isolated location.

December   The Kiplings travel to South Africa on the *RMS*

Tantallon. They go to Woolsack, their new home, which has been named after a previous owner of the lands on which it stands, Mr Wools-Sampson. (As a colonel, Wools-Sampson will raise and command Imperial Light Horse in the Second Boer War.) The Kiplings will live in Woolsack for several months each year between 1901 and 1908. They will see Cecil Rhodes almost every day. They will also cultivate friendships with Baden-Powell, Dr Jameson, and H. A. Gwynne. At Woolsack, in the years to come, RK will write some of the *Just So Stories*, some of *Puck of Pook's Hill* and *Rewards and Fairies*.

A lunatic, believing that RK is the reincarnation of his enemy, follows RK from England to Cape Town and tries to shoot him. RK gives him whisky, and the would-be assassin falls asleep. (In later years the man will dog RK's footsteps, and eventually fire a revolver at RK as he emerges from the Athenaeum. RK takes steps to have him locked up. He dies in prison. RK sends a large wreath to his funeral.)

1901

Kim runs serially in *McClure's Magazine*, 1900–1, and in *Cassell's Magazine*, 1901; both American and British editions of the book version appear in this year.

RK and Carrie advise Cecil Rhodes about his plans to endow scholarships to Oxford for men from the Dominions and the Colonies, the United States and Germany. They persuade Rhodes to increase the stipends from £250 to £300 by pointing out that students usually are unable to go home during school vacations.

April The RKs return to England.

25 May RK loses a lawsuit against G.P. Putnam's Sons for breach of copyright.

Summer The Catlins come over to England from the United States, and take the Kiplings to Paris.

July RK is on manoeuvres with the Fleet. Carrie goes through a period of deep depression.

1902

Just So Stories, consisting of 12 stories and 12 poems, is published.

January   RK writes 'The Islanders', an attack on the 'flannelled fools at the wicket or the muddied oafs at the goals', who do not understand the importance of national service. The poem is resented by many readers.

The same month, the Kiplings arrive in South Africa. Edgar Wallace interviews RK, and RK advises Wallace to write thrillers.

26 March   Cecil Rhodes dies, after murmuring, 'So little done – so much to do.' His body lies in state at Groote Schuur. RK advises Dr Jameson on the funeral ceremonies at Cape Town Cathedral, and the best means of handling the will; he writes verses for the Rhodes Memorial in Cape Town. Rhodes's body is taken to a grave in the Matoppos.

16 April   The Kiplings leave for England with JLK and Dr Jameson.

1 June   Peace is concluded in South Africa. Aunt Georgie, disgusted by the Treaty of Vereeniging, hangs a banner from a window of North End House that says, 'We have killed and also taken possession.' Young men of the village demonstrate angrily in front of the house. RK hurries over from the Elms and persuades them to go away.

8 June   F. Kinsey Peile's adaptation of 'The Man Who Was' as a one-act play opens at His Majesty's Theatre. Beerbohm Tree plays Limmason. He will keep the play in his repertory for several years.

10 June   RKs visit Bateman's, using a train and a hired fly to get to Burwash. RK's solicitor cousin, George Macdonald, negotiates the purchase of the house, the forge and 33 acres of land for £9300. Bateman's, built in 1634 by a Sussex ironmonger, has no bathroom, and no running water near the Kiplings' bedroom.

Later this month AMK comes to stay at Rottingdean. She brings Trix, who is now restored to health. Trix will later join her husband in India, until he retires from the service.

Summer The Kiplings complete the sale of Naulakha, in Brattleboro, to the Cabots. The price, $8000, is considerably less than its cost to RK. He invites Dr Conland to help himself to guns, rods and sporting-gear.

3 September The Kiplings move into Bateman's. RK orders from Messrs Gilkes and Gordon Ltd of Kendal a water turbine to drive a generator of 105/120 volts, 15 amperes, 1000 revolutions a minute, and its own switchgear. The installation will be completed in 1904; it will harness the River Dudwell to turn the mill-wheel and make electricity for the house. His adviser is Sir William Willcocks, who dammed the Nile at Aswan. The first visitors at Bateman's are Stanley and Cissie Baldwin and Hugh Poynter.

Autumn RK buys a 10-horsepower, two-cylinder 1902 Lanchester motor car and names it 'Jane Cakebread', after a notorious woman who has appeared in London courts 93 times on charges of disorderly behaviour. Lanchester will send RK various experimental models in the coming years, and he will send, in return, his comments on their performance.

December The Kiplings sail to Cape Town.

1903

Between 1903 and 1910 Trix, using the pseudonym of 'Mrs Holland', works under the direction of the British Society of Psychical Research, London; she develops a gift of crystal-gazing and automatic writing.

The Five Nations, containing 54 poems (28 of which are previously unpublished), is printed in both Britain and the United States.

RK writes 'Wireless', in which contact is made by aether with the past century.

7 February First performance of a stage adaptation of *The Light that Failed* by George Fleming (Constance Fletcher). Forbes-Robertson, Aubrey Smith and Gertrude Elliot play the leads.

11 March RK writes to E. Nesbit, telling her of his love for her Psammead stories, currently being published by *The Strand Magazine*. (He writes from the Woolsack.)

May He cultivates the acquaintance of Sir George Goldie and Sir Frederic Lugard, two shapers of Nigeria.

6 November A.J. Balfour writes to RK that the King 'would be pleased' to dub him a Knight Commander of the Order of St Michael and St George. 'You have always held up before your countrymen the Imperial ideal in its noblest shape.' The nomination is backed by the approval of Mr Lyttelton, recently made Secretary for the Colonies.

7 November RK declines. 'Such honours must continue outside my scheme of things.'

Later this year RK declines an invitation to join the royal party when the Prince of Wales (later George V) goes to India.

1904

January Publishes *The Muse among the Motors*, 14 poems written as parodies of the styles of various English and American poets. Several parodies will be added in later editions.

Easter Holidays The United Services College moves from Westward Ho! to Harpenden, Hertfordshire.

September *Traffics and Discoveries*, 11 stories and 11 poems, 'Mrs Bathurst' is written in the new style, i.e. more cryptic and denser in its suggestive meanings. RK writes to Mrs Hill that *Traffics and Discoveries* has really been put together for the purpose of carrying one political pamphlet, 'The Army of a Dream', and in that respect has failed. 'They' records some of RK's deep feeling of loss for Josephine. 'With the Night Mail', about an Atlantic Ocean crossing by air in the year 2000, becomes an instant science-fiction classic.

The Conservative Party in Edinburgh asks RK to stand for Parliament. He refuses.

RK begins *Puck of Pook's Hill*, basing parts of the stories on materials in the Sussex Records Office and on the Domesday book.

December   The Kiplings go to South Africa on the *RMS Armadale Castle*. On the 20th the ship hits a large fish, possibly a 'basking shark'.

1905

A quiet year, with only minor publications in book form: 'The Army of a Dream', reprinted from *Traffics and Discoveries*, and 'They', with illustrations by F.H. Townsend. RK continues work on the historical stories of *Puck of Pook's Hill*.

January–February   RK consults with Herbert Baker on the planning of the Rhodes Memorial at the Cape. G.P. Watts's statue of Physical Energy will be used because, as RK writes to Baker, it 'lies ready to our hands and will not delay the job. But that statue is the work of a great man grown old . . . .'

April   Lord Milner leaves South Africa to return to England, but his plans for gradual and steady development of enlightened white government cannot be realised because of the declining popularity of the Conservative Government in England.

December   Arthur Balfour resigns. A General Election, called for January 1906, will test the Conservative Government's mandate.

1906

Puck of Pook's Hill, 10 stories and 16 poems, is published. Aunt Aggie Poynter dies. RK calls her 'the dearest, sweetest of my mother's sisters'.

General Roberts forms the National Defence League to advocate national military service. RK vigorously supports the idea. At the end of Easter Term, the United Services College, a failing institution, moves from Harpenden, spends the summer at Richmond, then moves to Windsor, where it is absorbed by St Mark's School.

There is a Liberal landslide in the General Election. The House of Commons censures Milner. RK is upset by both developments.

1907

Collected Verse, containing all the poems in *Departmental Ditties, Ballads and Barrack-Room Ballads, The Seven Seas* and *The Five Nations,* is published.

May Stephen Leacock, a professor at McGill University, visits the Kiplings.

June RK accepts an offer of a doctorate from the University of Durham; then another from Oxford (in the same year as General Booth and Mark Twain); and, within a year, still another from Cambridge. He will become an Honorary Fellow of Magdalene College.

Summer RK sends a letter of condolence to the widow of Sergeant-Major George Schofield, the 'Weasel' of USC.

September John enters St Aubyns (also called Stanford's), a boarding-school in Rottingdean.

Autumn RK takes an Allen liner to Canada, on his only official tour of a Dominion. RK attends the graduation ceremony, addresses the graduating class, and accepts the degree of Doctor of Laws from McGill University. He lectures at several Canadian universities, and for three weeks travels through prairie country, Ottawa, Toronto, Regina, Calgary, and Vancouver. He also stays at Medicine Hat; in December 1910 he will express strong disapproval of a public vote to change the name of the town.

Winter The Secretary of the Swedish Academy writes RK a letter offering him the Nobel Prize for Literature: a gold medal, a diploma, and £7700. RK accepts, and is presented to the new king, Gustav V.

From 1907 on, he spends part of each winter at a 'sports' hotel in Switzerland, frequented by German officers.

1908

Letters to the Family, eight articles and seven poems written from notes taken during RK's trip to Canada, is published.

The Kiplings conclude their last visit to the Woolsack. RK is disgusted by increasing Afrikaner control, the 'handing over of a higher civilisation to a lower' in South Africa, and the censure of Lord Milner by the House of Commons. Even so, RK never surrenders his rights to the exclusive use of the Woolsack if ever he should return to South Africa. After his death the Woolsack becomes part of the Groote Schuur estate left by Rhodes to the South African Government.

RK warns England about German ambitions and a rising tide of militarism in that country.

On 1 October he lectures on 'A Doctor's Work' at the Middlesex Hospital Medical School.

Alfred Baldwin, Aunt Louisa's husband, dies.

The Kiplings visit Engelberg, Switzerland, for the first time, and will return to it – or to St Moritz – every year up to and including 1914, spending four to six weeks there.

1909

Actions and Reactions, eight stories and eight poems, and *Abaft the Funnel*, a collection mostly of turn-overs written for the *Civil and Military Gazette* in 1889, are published.

Between 1909 and 1914 RK serves as a propagandist for the Conservative Party. He gives lectures at meetings in London, and will speak on behalf of Max Aitken, a young Canadian (later Lord Beaverbrook), who will win his first election (Ashton-under-Lyne), in 1910. He develops a friendship with Bonar Law, who, like Aitken, is Canadian by origin.

RK writes his Boy Scouts' 'Patrol Song' for Baden-Powell, and visits an early Scout camp in the New Forest. The Wolf

Cub organisation for younger boys is indebted to the Mowgli stories.

1910

Rewards and Fairies continues the stories begun in *Puck of Pook's Hill*; the book contains 11 stories and 23 poems (one of which is 'If').

4 May 'Uncle Crom' dies at the age of 74.

Summer After the usual family holiday in Switzerland, the Kiplings travel to Vernet-les-Bains in the eastern Pyrenees to take the cure for Carrie.

RK attends the consecration of the Masonic 'Authors' Lodge' in London. He is also a member of the Motherland Lodge, and a Rosicrucian, being attached to the Metropolitan College. He is an honorary member of Canongate Kilwinning Lodge no. 2, Edinburgh (to which Robert Burns had also belonged as an honorary member).

Autumn RK's mother, AMK, falls ill. Trix, her husband and RK join JLK at the Gables, Tisbury. AMK dies on 23 November, and is buried at Tisbury.

Trix suffers another major breakdown (her third).

1911

RK contributes 23 poems to *A History of England*, by C.R.L. Fletcher.

January JLK dies at Clouds, Philip Webb's beautiful creation, built for the Percy Wyndhams; it stands near JLK's home in Tisbury. (The Wyndhams have become good friends of RK because of Ned, their brother-in-law.) RK, in Switzerland, is unable to arrive in time for the funeral.

Miss Sara Dunlop Anderson, formerly secretary to John Ruskin, and a secretarial assistant at various times to Burne-Jones,

Sir Henry Roscoe (chemist), and Thackeray's daughter, Lady Ritchie, stays on as RK's secretary. Miss Dorothy Ponton arrives at Bateman's to teach mathematics to John, and Latin and German to Elsie.

February   The Kiplings go to the Hôtel du Parc, Vernet-les-Bains, for the waters. Back in England, RK exchanges his Daimler for a Rolls-Royce. In this year he makes his first tour of France by motor. He visits Ireland, and is convinced that the Liberal Government should abandon the Home Rule Bill.

24 March   Meets Lord Roberts and General du Maurier at the Grand Hôtel du Portugal, Vernet-les-Bains.

September   John Kipling's eyesight prevents him from taking up Sir John Fisher's offer to nominate him to a naval cadetship. He goes instead to Wellington College, Berkshire, and is placed in the bottom form but one (the Middle Fourth). He makes slow progress at academic studies.

Late in the year RK again declines an invitation to visit India with King George V.

25 December   The Kiplings, John, and Elsie, and Bonar Law and his six children, spend Christmas with the Aitkens.

1912

Songs from Books, a collection of the great majority of RK's poems, including verse headings, is published. Some short items are expanded into longer poems.

January   The Kiplings stay at the Grand Hotel, Engelberg.

March   The Kiplings visit Venice.

25 May   RK lectures to the Literary Society, Wellington College, on 'The Possible Advantages of Reading'.

Summer   The name of the United Services College is changed to the Imperial Service College after its amalgamation with St Mark's, Windsor.

26 November W.C. Crofts ('King' in *Stalky & Co.*) drowns off the coast of Sark, at the sheltered cove of Baie des Laches.

Perceval Landon – a 'Friend' of Bloemfontein days – is becoming the best friend of RK's middle years. RK builds a cottage for him at Keylands, on the Bateman's estate. The road leading to Keylands will not be completed until October 1913.

Edmund Gosse and others invite RK to become one of the founders of the British Academy. He refuses. Later, he will (twice) refuse nomination to the American Academy of Arts and Sciences.

1913

February The Kiplings travel to Egypt, and see the Nile Valley for the first time. RK calls on Lord Kitchener in Cairo, and forms an unfavourable impression.

22 April *The Harbour Watch*, a one-act play written by RK, is produced at the Royalty Theatre, London. Edward Glass, the drunken Royal Marine, is played by G.F. Tully. Pyecroft is an important character. Vedrenne and Eadie's production – even though it is restricted to matinée performances – is not a great success. However, it is revived on 15 September, again as a curtain-raiser to St John Hankins' posthumous play *Thompson*.

August RK visits Aldershot to attend Summer Manoeuvres, and to become familiar with the men and planes of the Royal Flying Corps. He and Gwynne stay at Queen's Hall, Farnborough.

1914

3 March RK, along with 19 others, including Lord Milner and Lord Roberts, signs a letter to various newspapers announcing the formation of the British Covenant, which protests against the Home Rule Bill and pledges to prevent it from being enacted.

RK, along with Lord Astor, heads fund contributions that total £30,000.

April John Kipling leaves Wellington College in the Middle Second. He goes to an Army crammer, i.e. a private coaching-establishment, in Bournemouth.

5 May RK is elected to 'The Club', which dates back to Dr Johnson's time.

16 May RK makes a public speech to 10,000 Unionists on the Common at Tunbridge Wells; this savage attack on Liberals is strongly resented by many voters.

Late Spring – early Summer RK is made an honorary member of 'The Goat', the rendezvous of naval officers on leave in London. Later he donates a suitably mounted goat's head for the wall of the main room (he buys it from a taxidermist).

John Kipling is baptized into the Church of England at the age of 16. He has strongly insisted on it, much to his father's surprise. The Kiplings act as his sponsor.

The correspondence with Sir William Osler (at whose home he had stayed when waiting for the honorary-degree ceremonies at Oxford in 1907) becomes one of RK's great pleasures.

The RKs tour France.

4 August Great Britain declares war on Germany. RK writes 'For All We Have and Are', a rousing call to arms.

10 August RK leaves again for France. On board the ship that takes him across the Channel, he talks to Princess Victoria of Schleswig-Holstein. In Paris he visits Clemenceau, whom he met on an earlier occasion; he dislikes Briand; he meets General Nivelle. He sees Soissons while it is being shelled. He travels on to Rheims, Epernay, Verdun, and Thom.

14 September John Kipling reports for duty with the Second Battalion, Irish Guards. His commission has been secured for him by Lord Roberts, at the request of RK.

Sir Edward Grey threatens to resign if the British government sponsors RK's projected trip to the United States: 'For otherwise all my efforts to keep the goodwill of the United States will be useless.'

September Carrie keeps busy with aid to the Belgian refugees. She works for the Red Cross, sending piles of linen to the London Hospital. Trix falls ill again. RK suffers a (temporary) partial paralysis of facial muscles.

December RK receives an offer to accept the hospitality of French General Headquarters, so that he may interview generals and write a history of the Battle of Ypres (Oct–Nov). He refuses the invitation.

Christmas The Kiplings go to Aitken's house, Cherkley, in Leatherhead, Surrey.

1915

France at War, six articles from the London *Daily Telegraph* and the *New York Sun* (Sep 1915), is published. So is *The Fringes of the Fleet*, a collection of six articles written at the request of the Ministry of Information.

Spring RK supports a recruiting-campaign by delivering a strong anti-German speech at Southport, Lancashire, that attracts several thousand listeners in Lord Street.
 Several New Army officers are billeted for a while at Bateman's. RK offers Bateman's to the War Office for use as a hospital, but the offer is not accepted.

17 August John Kipling leaves England, and goes with the Irish Guards to France.

September RK visits the ships of the Dover Patrol, and of the Harwich Flotilla.

27 September The Irish Guards are thrown into a gap at the Battle of Loos, which ends with 20,000 British dead. John Kipling, in command of No. 5 Platoon, Second Battalion, is wounded, and listed as missing. RK is to continue inquiries –

on the forlorn chance that John has been taken prisoner – for two years. Finally, Sergeant Farrell of the Irish Guards tells them how John died. RK will pay a British gardener (employed by the War Graves Commission) to sound the Last Post at the Menin Gate every night in remembrance. This rite will continue until 1940, when the Germans overrun France.

1916

Sea Warfare, three series of articles written on behalf of the Ministry of Information, is published.

The Kiplings visit Bath, and an important friendship with George Saintsbury develops. Saintsbury is living in Bath in retirement. He will dedicate *Notes from a Cellar-Book* to RK.

Frank Doubleday suggests that RK visit the United States 'on a mission of friendship and goodwill', but RK refuses the offer.

1917

A Diversity of Creatures, 14 stories and 14 poems, is published. Sir Max Aitken – who will become Lord Beaverbrook in this year – attempts unsuccessfully to enlist RK in the Ministry of Information.

Mid-January RK accepts an offer to write the history of the Irish Guards. This requires conscientious research. Many of John's fellow officers will come to Bateman's to be interviewed.

May RK is appointed a Companion of Honour without his knowledge. He expresses his annoyance to Bonar Law: 'How would you like it if you woke up and found they had made you Archbishop of Canterbury?'

Mid-May He stays at the Grand Hotel, Rome, while travelling to the Italian front. He will visit Modane and Udine. His account will be published as *The War in the Mountains*.

September Sir Fabian Ware comes to Bateman's to invite RK – 'the soldiers' poet', as Lord Derby names him – to become a member of the Imperial War Graves Commission. RK will perform his duties as a Commissioner for the rest of his life. He helps to originate the plan to bury an unknown British soldier in Westminster Abbey.

He visits Winchester to see US soldiers in British training-camps.

Dr Jameson invites him to become a Rhodes Trustee, and to judge which worthy students shall receive Rhodes Scholarships.

26 November Dr Jameson dies.

1918

The Graves of the Fallen, a description of the work of the Imperial War Graves Commission, is published, as are British and American editions of the poem 'The Irish Guards', with its haunting refrain.

> *For where there are Irish there's memory undying,*
> *And when we forget, it is Ireland no more!*
> *Ireland no more!*

This poem is set to music by Edward German.

11 November RK learns from the ringing of church bells that the Armistice has been signed.

19 November RK meets the Prince of Wales. On this date he proposes the text for all altars in British cemeteries: 'Their Name Liveth for Evermore.'

Late December RK meets T.E. Lawrence of Arabia. Frank Doubleday introduces them to each other. RK regards Lawrence as the most romantic figure produced by the war.

27 December RK meets President Woodrow Wilson at Buckingham Palace. During this winter H. Rider Haggard comes to Bateman's from his new winter home at St Leonard's, and thinks that RK looks aged and ill.

1919

Miss Dorothy Ponton serves as RK's secretary from 1919 to 192ᵥ.
The Years Between, containing 45 poems and a collection of epitaphs, is published. This collection will be expanded later in the year to include 'The Muse among the Motors.'
Rudyard Kipling's Verse, Inclusive Edition, is published.

January Theodore Roosevelt dies. RK calls him 'Great Heart', not for the first time.
Carrie's mother dies.

February The Kiplings visit Bath, and RK is annoyed by a proposal, made by 'a Mr Brooking from Warrington', to start up a Kipling Society.

1 April RK attends dinner at 'The Club', Princes Hotel, Jermyn Street, and enjoys the company of Sir William Osler, the Archbishop of York (in the chair), Sir Henry Newbolt and John Buchan.

June RK suffers from severe eyestrain, caused by reading and correcting galley-proofs.

September RK goes to Scotland, and enjoys the quiet of Glenartney Forest.

1920

Letters of Travel, containing 'From Tideway to Tideway', 'Letters to the Family' and 'Egypt of the Magicians', is published. 'Brazilian Sketches' will be added to the volume in the collected editions.
RK contributes three of the 15 odes written by various scholars for the volume *Horace, Odes, Book V*, published by Basil Blackwell in England, and through the courtesy of the Colorado Yale Alumni Association Fund in the United States.

February RK takes Carrie to see 'the House of Desolation' in Southsea, where he lived with the Holloways.

2 February Aunt Georgie dies as a consequence of catching a severe cold.

May–June RK supervises the casting of John Kipling's memorial in bronze. It is placed in the church at Burwash.

July The University of Edinburgh awards him a doctorate.

Autumn On a motoring-tour of France, RK visits 30 cemeteries, and goes to see Chalk-Pit Wood, where John Kipling was killed (1915). He also visits Popperinghe and Arras.
  RK works with H. Rider Haggard in the Liberty League, an association formed to warn English men and women of the dangers of Russian Bolshevism.

1921

Lord Stamfordham, Private Secretary to the King, asks RK if he would accept nomination to the Order of Merit. RK declines, but suggests that the King visit the graves of the British dead in the Great War, a suggestion to which the King responds positively.
  André Chevillon brings a message from the University of Paris: RK has been offered a doctorate. RK will go there late in the year (Nov), and accept another doctorate from Strasbourg; he will be fêted by the Chamber of Deputies, and received by the President of the Republic.
  During the year he is troubled by unpleasant internal symptoms that are diagnosed by various doctors as gastritis, internal chill, an irritated stomach, adhesion of the liver and colon, etc. Sir John Bland-Sutton believes that the problem is due to septic foci in RK's teeth, and recommends that all of RK's teeth be removed. Although this is done, RK's medical problems continue, and will worsen in 1922.
  RK is disappointed by Pathé's film version of 'Without Benefit of Clergy'.
  The Kiplings enjoy holidaying at Hyères, and during their holiday at Cannes RK meets Bonar Law.
  The Kiplings sail on the *SS Timgad* from Marseilles to Algiers, and stay in that city for four weeks.
  At Bateman's, RK purchases a 1920 Rolls-Royce Silver Ghost,

40/50 horsepower, Series 6VE. He will run it until 1928. After his ownership ends, the car will be purchased by the Howra Temple Trust in Calcutta, India, where it will be used on ceremonial occasions.

1922

March   The Kiplings embark for Gibraltar on the *SS Ormuz*.

11 May   RK is instructed to meet King George V at Vlamertinge, near Ypres. Field-Marshal Haig joins the party. The King delivers a speech that RK has written for him.

13 May   RK attends a ceremony at Terlincthun, near Boulogne. He sees a memorial to 'Gunga-Din, stretcher-bearer', among other Indian graves.

Summer   RK drafts a political manifesto for the Conservative Party.

11 September   The anti-British *New York World* prints the text of a supposed interview with RK by Mrs Clare Sheridan, who has had tea at Bateman's. She is the daughter of the Frewens, who are neighbours of the Kiplings in Burwash. RK disavows the inflammatory remarks he is purported to have made about US–British relationships, and both the French and British governments brand the interview as not being authentic.

October   The Kiplings visit London. Stanley Baldwin visits him at Brown's Hotel. RK's gastric pains are so severe that Sir John Bland-Sutton operates. The King and Queen send their sympathy.

November   RK, ill again, goes to a nursing-home in Fitzroy Square. An old ulcer has flared up; he undergoes treatment for gastritis, and he is placed on a heavy dose of Epsom salts every morning; his bowels must be washed out twice a day; he can eat no solid food. But X-rays indicate that what he has feared (cancer) is groundless. He returns to Bateman's in time for Christmas.

1923

The Irish Guards in the Great War, a two-volume work undertaken as a final tribute to John Kipling, is published, as is *Land and Sea Tales*, a collection of 11 stories and eight poems.

The film scenario of *The Gate of a Hundred Sorrows* is written by 'an American' under RK's instructions at Bateman's. (A synopsis of this script will be published in *Rudyard Kipling's World*, by Thurston Hopkins, in 1925.) In the script Mother Maturin is a character who 'makes a home' for an alcoholic named Andrew MacIntosh.

February RK attends the annual dinner of the Royal College of Surgeons, and praises the skill of the surgeon in a speech, 'Surgeons of the Soul'.

April The Kiplings go to the Hotel California, Cannes, and enjoy their stay on the Riviera.

October RK is elected Lord Rector of the University of St Andrews and delivers his Rectorial Address.

24 October Bonar Law dies.

1924

RK is invited a second time to accept nomination to the Order of Merit, and again he declines. He accepts a doctorate from the University of Athens.

22 October Elsie Kipling marries Captain George Bambridge, who has served in the Irish Guards. The wedding takes place at St Margaret's, Westminster. She will live abroad with him for many years; he will serve as Honorary Attaché at the British Embassy in Madrid, and then at diplomatic postings in Brussels and Paris. Neither RK nor Carrie is enthusiastic about the match.

20 November   RK is entered in the Candidates' Book of the Beefsteak Club, London. He is proposed by Sir Frederick Macmillan, his publisher, and seconded by Perceval Landon and Charles Whibley. He will become a member in 1925.

1925

The Kiplings tour the continent until 20 April. They visit Evreux, Dreux, Chartres, Périgueux, the caves of the Dordogne, and Lourdes.

14 May   H. Rider Haggard dies. This death takes place at almost the same time as that of Lord Milner. Lady Milner, who requests RK to write a biography of her husband, is gently refused.

16 May   Aunt Louie Baldwin dies.

June   RK reads his work aloud to 28 'Lower School Imps' of Eton College, at the request of A.B. Ramsay, the Master.

15 June   RK resigns from the Rhodes Trust because the Liberal Philip Kerr (later Marquess of Lothian) is appointed to a vacant place. Such an appointment, RK believes, is contrary to Rhodes's intentions for the Trust.

3 July   RK receives the freedom of the City of London.

31 August   The 'Actors Memorial' is dedicated in St Peter's Chapel, Holy Trinity Church, Stratford-on-Avon. RK's epitaph dedicated to the memory of the men of Stratford-on-Avon who were killed in the war, is on a grey marble tablet designed by Sir George Frampton.

1926

Debits and Credits, 14 stories and 21 poems, is published.

July   RK receives from Earl Balfour the Gold Medal of the Royal Society of Literature. The Medal has been awarded only three times before: to Sir Walter Scott, George Meredith and Thomas Hardy.

Various illnesses torment him during the year. Severe pneumonia, at one point, sends him to bed. Lord Dawson detects 'a flutter in his heart'.

December President Poincaré receives RK on his visit to France. Next day, Clemenceau (who has retired from politics) also receives him.

1927

Rudyard Kipling's Verse (Inclusive Edition, 1884–1926), is published. This volume adds 35 poems to the edition of 1921, taken from *Land and Sea Tales*, *Debits and Credits* and *Songs of the Sea*. Six poems have not previously been collected.

Perceval Landon dies.

The Kipling Society, with 100 members, finally gets under way. (It has been gestating for eight years.) The devoted leaders of the new organisation are Mr J. H. C. Brooking, General Dunsterville ('Stalky'), and Major J. H. Beith ('Ian Hay'). Stalky agrees to serve as the first President. The Committee is composed of Mr Brooking, George Beresford ('M'Turk') and Sir George MacMunn. RK writes, 'if it has got to be done let it be *as private and quiet as possible.*'

Winter The Kiplings sail from Southampton to Brazil aboard the *RMSP Andes*, arriving in Rio on 13 February. RK will describe his trip in seven travel letters written to the *Morning Post* in London and to *Liberty* in the United States. These, in turn, will be collected in vol. XXIV of the Burwash Edition. RK visits Copacabana Beach in Rio; then travels by steamer to Santos, a port 250 miles south-west of Rio, and another 50 miles on to Saõ Paulo. Although these *Brazilian Sketches* are vague on details of what RK does and sees during this brief visit, three unusual localities – a power-house, a snake farm, and a coffee plantation with 500,000 bushes – are described at some length.

5 October RK tells Lord Lloyd that a speech by Lord Birkenhead, on the occasion of the unveiling of the war memorial to the

Indian dead at Neuve Chapelle, is the finest funeral oration since Gettysburg.

At about the same time, RK meets T.E. Lawrence at a dinner in Brown's Hotel, and finds that his early admiration of Lawrence's exploits has changed to a dislike of Lawrence's personality.

1928

31 addresses delivered by RK between 1906 and 1927 are collected in *A Book of Words*, and published.

16 January Thomas Hardy is buried in Westminster Abbey, and RK serves as one of the six pall-bearers, along with Sir James Barrie, John Galsworthy, Sir Edmund Gosse, A.E. Housman and George Bernard Shaw.

20 January Edward Kay Robinson, editor of the *Civil and Military Gazette* when RK was his assistant, dies at Hampton Wick at the age of 72.

June Carrie breaks down. Lord Dawson puts her on a rigorous diet. Her health has been deteriorating for several years, but matters are complicated by her threats of self-violence. She is increasingly concerned about RK's privacy, but her rheumatism and gout are crippling her; she is a confirmed diabetic; and she is unable to lead as active a life as she would like. Her treatment: baths and repeated massages.

11 July RK buys a dark-green Phantom I 40/50 horsepower Rolls-Royce for £2833 18s. 6d. He exults in the fact that it can do 114 miles in 160 minutes. (This is the car, in restored condition, on exhibition today at Bateman's.) RK will run it until 1932.

28 October William Thacker Spink, RK's first publisher, dies at the age of 73.

10 November RK contributes 'We have served our day' to a panel in the Hall of the Institute of Journalists, Tudor Street,

London, as a memorial to journalists of the British Empire who died in the Great War.

1929

Poems 1886–1929 is published in three volumes.

RK becomes godfather to the son of Maurice Hammoneau, whose life was saved during the war by a copy of *Kim*; it stopped a German bullet. RK insists that both the book and the Croix de Guerre (sent to him by Hammoneau) belong to the child.

RK presents to his Mother Lodge – Lodge Hope and Perseverance – at Lahore a gavel made of stone from the quarries supposed to have been used in the construction of King Solomon's Temple at Jerusalem.

February   At the Semiramis Hotel, Cairo, RK renews his acquaintance with A.E.W. Mason, and enthusiastically praises Mason's *The Prisoner in the Opal*. He also advises Mason on the plot of *The Three Gentlemen*.

February–March   RK visits Sinai, and is fascinated by the fact that one Englishman – Claude Scudamore Jarvis (1879-1953) – governs the entire peninsula.

5 October   RK makes the principal speech, 'School Experiences', at King's School, Canterbury, at the opening of the new Junior School. Lady Milner and the Archbishop of Canterbury are present.

1930

Thy Servant a Dog, Told by Boots is published, and sells 100,000 copies in six months.

Late February   The RKs sail for the West Indies with Helen Hardinge, Lady Milner's daughter.

1 March   They land in Jamaica. RK refuses the Governor's invitation to visit him. Carrie collapses with appendicitis; she must be taken to a hospital in Bermuda. The following three months (March–May) are RK's longest separation from Carrie.

1 June Determined not to set foot again in the United States, RK sets out with Carrie for Halifax, Nova Scotia, from where they travel to Montreal and then on to England. (From Bermuda the normal route to England would be via the United States.)

4 August RK attends the unveiling of the memorial at Dud Corner Cemetery, Loos. Although scheduled to speak, he is overcome by emotion, and he asks General Sir Nevil Macready to deliver the address.

7 December Three lines from 'A Song of the English (England's Answer)' are engraved on a wall memorial at St Mildred's Church, Bread Street, London, in honour of Admiral Arthur Phillip, the first governor of Australia.

1931

Late February The Kiplings go to Egypt, and stay till April; they visit Palestine as well.

June They visit Paris.
    RK accepts the invitation of Lord Crewe and the executive committee of the British Institute in Paris to become a member of the London Committee.

2 July RK is the guest of honour of the France Grand Bretagne Association at its annual banquet held at the Circle Interalliée.

September They visit Oxford.
    RK becomes increasingly angry at what he considers Stanley Baldwin's socialism.

6 October He refuses the invitation of Sydney Cockerell to write a book about Lady Burne-Jones, his 'beloved Aunt' who died in 1920. (This is Aunt Georgie.)

1932

Limits and Renewals, containing 14 stories and 19 poems, is published. Three of the stories and 18 of the poems are printed for the first time. This book will be his last collection.

Miss Cecily Nicholson, sent to the Kiplings by an employment agency, becomes RK's private secretary (1932–9), and later will serve in a similar capacity at Wimpole Hall with Mrs Elsie Bambridge (1940–54).

James, RK's Aberdeen terrier, dies; RK is deeply moved.

His gross income for this year is £32,821. On this he pays income tax of £7989, plus approximately £9000 in super-tax.

The King, in his address to the Empire, quotes RK's words. The fact that RK writes several other speeches for the King is a well-kept secret.

RK purchases a 20/25 horsepower Rolls-Royce. (This will be his last car.)

29 May RK is elected to an Honorary Fellowship, Magdalene College, Cambridge, on the first day of full term. He is admitted in chapel before evensong.

1933

April Dr Roux, in Paris, finally diagnoses RK's health problem as duodenal ulcers. He recommends treatment that, to some extent, alleviates the severe pains that RK has been experiencing after meals.

Spring–Summer RK becomes a member of the India Defence League, and is elected a Vice-President.

The Kiplings visit Wimpole Hall, 8 miles south of Cambridge, (which the Bambridges have rented from Lord Clifden) at least twice (30 May and 7 July). The Bambridges will purchase Wimpole Hall in 1938.

Summer The Kiplings rent a villa near Cannes.

RK and G. K. Chesterton are filmed (in sound) making a speech at a banquet at the Canadian Authors' Association.

24 June RK is unanimously elected a Foreign Associate Member of the Académie des Sciences et Politiques. M. Camille Barrère, formerly the French Ambassador to Italy, proposes him.

October *Verse, Inclusive Edition, 1885–1932*, the last edition of poems proof-read by RK, is published.

Winter *His Apologies*, a silent film based on RK's poem (1932), traces the life of a dog from birth till the moment he is shot by his master because he is so old. (The studio responsible is Famous Films.) A prize-winning Scottish terrier from Reading is used as principal actor. RK will see this film at a trade show (1 Nov 1935).

1934

1 January The Kiplings leave the Grand Pump Room, Bath.
The same month, Frank Nelson Doubleday dies at the age of 72.

Summer The Kiplings spend three months in Hyères and Cannes; a fortnight in Jersey (where Carrie undergoes treatment prescribed by Sir Herbert Barker); several days at the Grand Pump Room, Bath (for the same purpose); a weekend at Deal; another at Cirencester; and so on.
RK is offered one of the higher ranks in the Légion d'Honneur; he declines.

1935

The *Morning Post* reports that six of RK's works are being filmed by British and American studios: in the United States, *Kim* and *Captains Courageous* (MGM), and *The Light that Failed* (Paramount); in England, *Toomai of the Elephants* (directed by Robert Flaherty for London Film Productions), *Soldiers Three* (Gaumont-British) and *His Apologies* (already released; see 1933).
RK helps to greater or lesser degree in the preparation of all the scripts. He even works for two months with Colonel A.R. Rawlinson on a screenplay based on the *Soldiers Three* stories (not the one ultimately completed), and another scenario based on the

tale 'Aunt Ellen'. Perhaps the greatest effort made to guarantee authenticity is made by the producers of *Soldiers Three*: battle scenes are staged near Landikotal at the summit of the Khyber Pass, and the uniforms are as close as possible to those used in the 1890s. *Toomai of the Elephants*, for which Alexander Korda pays £5000 to RK, will be renamed *Elephant Boy*.

February The Kiplings begin a three-month stay in Cannes, and will return to Cannes in August. The Kiplings visit the Stanley Baldwins in Paris.

RK attends the Naval Review with Sir Percy Bates, the ship-owner, and watches the event from on board the *Berengaria*. The design of the *Queen Mary* fascinates him, and he writes several technical letters to Sir Percy about its construction.

The Kiplings go to Marienbad so that Carrie may 'take the cure'.

June RK, Dunsterville and Beresford ('Stalky & Co.') meet at a reunion of two dozen Old Boys of USC in London.

Summer RK writes a 'Just So' story, 'Ham and the Porcupine', for Princess Elizabeth's Gift Book.

1 August RK begins to write *Something of Myself*. The title has been suggested to him by Sir Alfred Webb-Johnson, President of the Royal College of Surgeons. (In this work, to be published after his death, RK does not mention Flo Garrard, Mrs Hill, the death of either Josephine or John Kipling, and what went wrong in Vermont.)

13 August RK goes to Eastbourne to meet 84 boys and girls from secondary schools in Canada, who are visiting England for six weeks under the auspices of the Overseas Education League.

Autumn RK and Lord Hailsham are elected to fill two vacancies in the Chamberlain Club.

November RK votes in the General Election; he is disgusted that Stanley Baldwin earns a huge majority.

RK visits Wimpole Hall, Cambridgeshire, presumably after the Bambridges have decided to purchase it.

1936

January The Kiplings make plans to go to Cannes and join the Tauffliebs for a winter stay. They come to Brown's Hotel for a few days before leaving.

9 January RK signs his will.

12 January The RKs go to Hampstead to visit George Bambridge.

13 January RK haemorrhages in the night; his gastric ulcer is the culprit, and he is rushed to Middlesex Hospital. His doctor, Sir Alfred Webb-Johnson, examines him at 3 a.m., then operates. Carrie and Elsie are warned of the riskiness of the operation.

18 January Peritonitis sets in; RK dies at 10.10 a.m.

20 January RK is cremated in secret at Golders Green Crematorium.

22 January The urn containing RK's ashes is moved to St Faith's Chapel in Westminster Abbey. King George V, who has died on the 20th, only two days after RK, lies in state in Westminster Hall. It is said that the King has died and taken his trumpeter with him.

23 January RK's ashes are interred in Poets' Corner, Westminster Abbey, next to the graves of Charles Dickens and Thomas Hardy. His pall-bearers are a Prime Minister, Stanley Baldwin (RK's cousin), Admiral of the Fleet Sir Roger Keyes, Field Marshal Sir A. Montgomery-Massingberd, Professor J. W. Mackail, Mr H. A. Gwynne, Sir Fabian Ware, Mr A. B. Ramsay and Mr A. P. Watt. Among the family present are Mrs Kipling, with her son-in-law and daughter, Captain and Mrs George Bambridge; Mrs Stanley Baldwin; Miss Betty Baldwin and Mr Oliver Baldwin; Mr A.W. Baldwin; Miss Florence Macdonald; and Mrs Thirkell. Miss Cecily Nicholson (RK's secretary) sits with the family. A distinguished list of diplomats, ambassadors and ministers, publishers, editors, and representatives of various institutions and organisations with which RK has associated himself, attend the interment, as do a substantial number of the members of the Kipling Society. The service is performed by the Dean of Westminster and the Abbey clergy.

After the service, a procession moves past the grave. 'Recessional' is sung. Also sung is a hymn he chose some time before, 'Abide with Me'.

Carrie collapses for a short time, and is advised by her doctors to go to the South of France (Feb–Mar). Her health remains poor; she will have several heart attacks before she dies. Though she visits London often, she never will return to Brown's Hotel.

7 April   RK's estate is reported by *The Times* as £155,228 gross. The sum is not an accurate picture of his real wealth, however, inasmuch as he earned more than a million pounds in his lifetime, and transferred before his death very large sums to his daughter.

25 July   Mr and Mrs F. Cabot Holbrook, owners of RK's former home Naulahka in Brattleboro, Vt, invite public inspection of the home every weekday afternoon 'for a small fee'.

30 July   In Vermont, Beatty Balestier dies.

Afterwards

1937   *Something of Myself*, edited by Carrie, H. A. Gwynne and Sir Alfred Webb-Johnson (knighted in 1936), is published.
Stephen Wheeler, Editor of the *Civil and Military Gazette* when RK worked in Lahore, dies in January.

1938   Flo Garrard dies on 31 January, and George C. Beresford dies of heart failure on 21 February.

1939   The Sussex Edition, in 35 volumes, is published. Because RK prepared the final revised text, this must be considered the most authoritative edition. (Although Macmillan identifies all the volumes as having been published in 1937, only some of them were.)
On 6 March the Foundation Stone of the RK Memorial Buildings at the Imperial Service College, Windsor, is laid by Princess Alice, Countess of Athlone.
Carrie turns over Bateman's to the National Trust, and dies there on 19 December.

1940   *Rudyard Kipling's Verse: Definitive Edition* is issued by Hodder and Stoughton in London, and by Doubleday, Doran and Co. in

New York. The book is authorised by Mrs Bambridge, but it does not contain a large number of poems included in Vol. XXV of the Sussex Edition.

1941 The Burwash Edition, published by Doubleday, Doran and Co., appears in 28 volumes; it follows the text of the Sussex Edition.

1942 Major General J.C. Rimington, CB, a fellow classmate of RK at the United Services College, dies on 30 April. In the same year, the Imperial Service College (successor of the USC) transfers from Windsor and, because the number of its students has been steadily declining, amalgamates with Haileybury. 30 of its 37 years with a separate identity as USC were spent at Westward Ho!

Lieutenant Colonel J.M. Fleming, late of the Indian Army and Trix's husband, dies at the age of 84.

1943 The Town Council of Windsor buys the Imperial Service College buildings – including the Kipling Memorial Hall, which cost £60,000 when it was built in 1938 – for £37,250.

Mrs Elizabeth Anne Macdonald, widow of the Rev Frederick W. Macdonald and RK's maternal aunt, dies at the age of 85.

Captain George Louis St Clair Bambridge, husband of RK's only surviving daughter, Elsie, dies at the age of 51.

1946 On 17 March, Major General L.C. Dunsterville, model for 'Stalky' and President of the Kipling Society, dies at the age of 80 in Torquay.

1948 Following the death of Earl Baldwin of Bewdley (Stanley Baldwin) on 14 December 1947, and his burial at Worcester Cathedral, there is a memorial service for him in Westminster Abbey in January.

On 25 October, Trix (Mrs Alice Macdonald Fleming) dies at West Coates, Edinburgh, at the age of 80.

1951 The film version of *Kim* opens at the Empire Theatre to mixed reviews.

1952 Edmonia Hill dies in Baltimore, Maryland.

1956 Florence Macdonald dies in January.

1961 Angela Thirkell, the daughter of J.W. Mackail and Margaret Burne-Jones, a woman regarded by RK as his favourite cousin, dies in January, at the age of 71.

1963 On 4 September the *Civil and Military Gazette* shuts down permanently in Lahore (now in Pakistan).

1969 Lieutenant Colonel R.S. Hawkins (Retired), a member of the Sussex Archaelogical Society, works with the Royal Electrical and Mechanical Engineers and the National Trust to renovate the turbine and the site of the mill at Bateman's. This work will be completed in 1973.

1976 On 24 May Mrs George Bambridge (Elsie Kipling) dies at the age of 80 in Edgecombe House (a nursing-home), Berkshire. She is buried on the 27th.

Among Those Who Knew Kipling

This listing of Kipling's family relations and acquaintances is necessarily briefer than it could be. I have not tried to prepare the usual biographical entry, but have rather attempted to indicate how the life of Rudyard Kipling intersected with each person named. This collection of information about Kipling's associates – some of whom were more intimate than others, to be sure, and some of whom did not know Kipling for more than a relatively brief period of time – offers convenient cross-references to people and events in the Chronology itself. I have attempted in this section to minimise the repetition of facts that have already appeared in the Chronology.

Kipling's enthusiasm for conversation and for making friends must impress all readers interested in his life. Kipling probably knew as many individuals in as many occupations and professions as any writer of his time. He was particularly good at securing the confidence of children, whom he took very seriously. The Visitors' Book at Bateman's, maintained faithfullly between 1902 and 1936, lists an astonishing number of names, not all known (or knowable) to the most assiduous researcher or biographer. Moreover, Kipling, while travelling, frequently chose not to reveal his identity; he was more interested in answers than in impressing anybody with his status. He needed information about geographical conditions, national characteristics, historical events: he saw himself as a chronicler and an interpreter, and he chose not to make an issue of his fame. He was, in several respects, a modest man.

I hope that such a sampling of those who knew him will prove both useful and interesting to readers of this Chronology.

Allen, Sir George (1831–1900), established the *Pioneer* at Allahabad, the railway centre of India, and made it a successful all-India newspaper. He encouraged the parents of RK to write columns and submit chatty items for publication, and approved the hiring of RK at the *Civil and Military Gazette*; four years later, he decided to transfer him to Allahabad. At a critical moment in his life, debating whether to leave India, RK was encouraged by the commissioning, by Allen, of a series of travel sketches, to be written *en route* to England.

Anderson, Sara Dunlop (1854–1942), served as RK's private secretary during several years of the twentieth century. Before coming to Bateman's she had been John Ruskin's secretary, and had held a number of other important and confidential secretarial positions.

Baden-Powell, Robert Stephenson Smyth Baden-Powell, Baron (1857–1941), founded the Boy Scouts and Girl Guides. RK's *Land and Sea Tales for Scouts and Guides* (1923) is in large part a celebration of the ethos of this movement, and Baden-Powell's indebtedness to the *Jungle Books* can hardly be overestimated. RK wrote 'Patrol Song' on Baden-Powell's behalf (1909). The two men met at the Cape in 1901, and kept in touch through correspondence. As Scouting evolved (1907–8), RK called himself, proudly, 'Commissioner of Boy Scouts', went to Scout rallies, and visited at least one Scout camp.

Baldwin, Alfred (1841–1908), husband of Louisa Macdonald and father of Stanley Baldwin, who was to become Prime Minister, was a very successful ironmaster who became the Chairman of the Great Western Railway. In 1871 he wanted to take in Trix, as a playmate of his son; but, because of Ruddy's reputation as a hell-raiser, he proposed that RK spend his years away from India at the homes of his uncle Burne-Jones and his uncle Fred Macdonald. The problems inherent in separating the children from each other led to the decision of RK's parents to send them instead to a boarding-house, a practice fairly common among parents who wanted their children to escape the heat and fevers of India during their most vulnerable years.

Baldwin, Arthur Windham, 3rd Earl Baldwin (1904-1977), second son of the 1st Earl Baldwin of Bewdley, was a cousin of RK. He worked in the family steel business, and later became a Director of the Great Western Railway. His book *My Father: The True Story* was a spirited defence of his father. He served several years as President of the Kipling Society.

Baldwin, Louisa Macdonald (1845–1925), known as 'Aunt Louie', married a rich ironmaster, Alfred Baldwin, and became the mother of Stanley Baldwin, future Prime Minister and (until political differences soured the relationship) a close friend of RK. She suggested the name of Rudyard (after a reservoir lake, important as the scene of first encounter in the courtship of JLK and AMK). RK confided in her, and some of his chattiest and most poignant letters are addressed to her. It may well be that Aunt Louie lengthened RK's stay in 'the House of Desolation' at Southsea, because she thought well of Mrs Holloway ('a very nice woman indeed'). Despite this misjudgement RK never held a grudge against her, and he deeply mourned her passing.

Baldwin, Stanley (1867-1947), later 1st Earl Baldwin of Bewdley, was the son of Louisa Macdonald (Aunt Louie) and Alfred Baldwin. He came into RK's life at a particularly difficult moment, and helped RK to regain his emotional stability: immediately after RK had been rescued from Mrs Holloway in Southsea. He and Trix enjoyed themselves – literally recuperated – on a farm in Epping Forest, while RK and Stanley quickly formed a mischief-hunting team. From Lahore (1884) RK wrote to Miss Edith Macdonald, 'I'd give something to be in the Sixth at Harrow as [Stanley] is, with a University Education to follow'; but that was not to be, because of JLK's limited funds. In later years RK envied Stanley Baldwin's 'wonderful voice' and 'personal popularity', though, from the 1920s on, he disagreed strongly with his cousin's politics. This disagreement did not much affect their personal relations. RK had a hand in editing (even writing) some of Stanley's speeches. Stanley experienced several times the pleasure of offering honours to RK, and the disappointment of being turned down.

Balestier, Caroline Starr, Carrie's grandmother, was the descendant of General Roger Wolcott, second-in-command at the Battle of Louisburg (1745); Oliver Wolcott, who signed the Declaration of Independence for Connecticut (1776), fought at Saratoga, and became Governor of Connecticut (1796–7); and Oliver II, who succeeded Alexander Hamilton as Secretary of the Treasury and then served as Governor of Connecticut (1817–27).

Caroline married Joseph Balestier in the 1830s, then moved to Vermont (from Chicago), and settled in Brattleboro (1872). She continued to keep a house in New York City for many years. She was always known as 'Madam Balestier', until she died in 1901. Wolcott was her eldest grandson, and Carrie her eldest grand-daughter.

Balestier, Wolcott (1861–91), moved with ease from an incomplete education at Cornell and a sojourn of several months in the American West (Colorado) to a position as agent for the New York firm of Lovell and Co. Shortly after Wolcott went to England to negotiate royalty contracts with English authors for publication of their works in the United States, he met RK at a party in the home of Mrs Humphry Ward, a well-known novelist (Mar 1890). Wolcott, knowing the American market, may have advised RK to write a happy ending to the version of *The Light that Failed* that appeared in *Lippincott's Monthly Magazine* (Jan 1891) and in the first English edition; RK respected Wolcott's literary judgement, and wanted very much for his novel to succeed. RK's collaboration with Wolcott on *The Naulahka*, his next novel, divided the story in terms of locale: RK wrote the chapters about India, Wolcott those dealing with the American West. Wolcott introduced RK to his sister in his office at Dean's Yard, at Westminster Abbey; he encouraged their courtship, though at first it did not proceed smoothly. Wolcott did not realise how much his relentless schedule had overworked his weak constitution. Shortly after he moved to the Continent on an assignment for Heinemann – he intended to publish cheap English-language editions of English and American works in European printing-houses, competing with Tauchnitz, and at the same time cutting distribution costs – he died in Dresden of typhoid fever. (He probably picked up the disease in Dean's Yard.) Fortunately, his mother and two sisters were able to be with him in his final moments. Henry James, greatly impressed by Wolcott's character and ability, travelled to Dresden to help make final arrangements. RK, learning in Lahore of Wolcott's death (Dec 1891) travelled with remarkable speed (14 days) back to London to comfort the Balestiers. Less than a month after Wolcott's death RK married his sister, Carrie, at All Souls', Langham Place. Despite a wide variety of male friendships in the half-century that followed, nobody replaced Wolcott in RK's affections and memories.

Bambridge, Captain George Louis St Clair (1893–1943), married RK's daughter Elsie in 1924. He served in the Irish Guards during the Great War; knew John Kipling as a fellow soldier; and earned for himself the Military Cross. He served as an attaché in various British embassies: Madrid, Brussels and Paris. At the invitation of Lord Derby, he joined the committee of the United Associations of Great Britain and France.

Beresford, George C. (1864–1938) was one of the immortal trio in *Stalky & Co.*, the other two being RK ('Gigs') and L.C. Dunsterville ('Stalky'). As 'M'Turk', he helped to carry out Stalky's inventive schemes. His personality was that of a free-speaking Celt. He spent four years in India, as an engineer; he had serious interests in art, and exhibited at the Royal Academy; he was also a close friend of Sir William Orpen. He developed real talents in photography, and had considerable skill as a dealer in antiques. He served for more than a decade as a hard-working member of the Kipling Society.

Besant, Sir Walter (1836–1901), wrote the novel *All in a Garden Fair* (1883), which pleased Kipling greatly at the time he read it in 1886, when he was developing his own creative talents with 'turn-overs' for E. Kay Robinson. Kipling read the book several times, and took to heart the distinction that Besant drew between the East, which is slow to change, and the West (more specifically, London), which benefits from new discoveries, theories and men at a very rapid rate; it helped Kipling to decide on his return to England in the near future, where he could win a literary reputation among readers whose opinions he respected. The novel also expressed a number of views about unscrupulous publishers (a lifelong concern of Besant, who helped to found the Society of Authors in 1884) that Kipling found ample reason to endorse during the 1890s. Besant supported Kipling for membership in the Savile Club, and offered literary advice that Kipling respected (and sometimes followed). A difference of opinion over the integrity of Harper and Brothers as a publishing-house led Kipling to list Besant, along with Thomas Hardy and William Black, as pirates in 'The Rhyme of the Three Captains', but this controversy soon blew over, and they resumed their friendship. Besant introduced Kipling to A.P. Watt, the literary agent, who promptly untangled many of the copyright problems arising from unauthorised publication of Kipling's works. Besant praised 'Recessional' as the superb creation of 'genius'.

Blackwood, Frederick Temple Hamilton-Temple, 1st Marquis of Dufferin and Ava (1826–1902), succeeded George Frederick Samuel Robinson, Lord Ripon, as the Governor-General of India on 13 December 1884, and retired from India in December 1888. During these years he did much to conciliate a population upset by the Ilbert Bill (which would have subjected Anglo-Indians to the verdicts of Indian judges) and by Lord Ripon's unfinished schemes of self-government for the Indians. RK reported many of his activities – for example, the reception of Abdur Rahman, the Amir of Afghanistan (Mar 1885) at Rawalpindi. At Simla the Viceroy cultivated the acquaintance of RK's parents, and said (more than once) that 'Dullness and Mrs Kipling cannot exist in the same room.' However, he nipped in the bud a romance between his son, Lord Clandeboye, and Trix, by sending his son, his aide-de-camp, back to England. He greatly admired RK's literary style. Late in 1890 Lord Dufferin, now the British Ambassador at Rome, invited RK to his villa at Sorrento. More important than his polite but ever-friendly social relations with RK, perhaps, was the service he rendered when he persuaded the new Viceroy of India to establish a pension for JLK, so that he might retire comfortably.

Bland-Sutton, Sir John (1855–1936), was probably the leading gynaecological surgeon of his day, and served as President of the Royal College of Surgeons (1923–6). His book *Tumours Innocent and Malignant* (1893) is his best-known work, and a classic of medical literature. His close friends included RK, who enjoyed his intellectual curiosity (and shared it: see *Something of Myself*, wherein is recounted an anecdote of the two men pursuing a reluctant pullet to investigate the workings of its gizzard). The only other doctor named in RK's autobiography is Dr Conland. Bland-Sutton is the original of Sir James Belton in 'The Tender Achilles'.

Brooking, J.H.C. (1871–1962), served as a sailor on at least one round-the-world voyage, then as an electrical engineer for fully 70 years. He helped to found both the Institution of Mining

Engineers and Electrical Engineers (1908) and the Institute of the
Rubber Industry (1921). He was the prime mover in the founding
of the Kipling Society (4 Feb 1927).

Buck, Sir Edward (1838–1916), was Secretary to the Government
of India, and RK was his guest frequently during his visits to Simla.
In this house, during the 1870s, Mme Blavatsky had produced
'manifestations' of the spiritual world; JLK had considered them
fakery; and it remained for Sir Edward to expose the tricks by
which she had persuaded an all-too-credulous public that she
possessed supernatural powers (1879).

Burne-Jones, Sir Edward (1833–98), known as 'Uncle Ned',
was a school-friend of Cormell Price (Uncle Crom), and this
was undoubtedly the key reason why the United Services College,
otherwise a most unlikely place for the visually handicapped RK,
was chosen by JLK and AMK for Ruddy's education. (USC
was also inexpensive.) The importance of the welcome given
by Burne-Jones and his loving wife, Aunt Georgie, cannot be
overestimated; their home, and their love, could always be
depended on. Moreover, RK's circle of friends included many
who had been introduced to him by Burne-Jones (for example,
Professor Charles Eliot Norton of Harvard). Burne-Jones identified
useful source-books for English history, which contributed to the
authenticity of *Puck of Pook's Hill* and *Rewards and Fairies*. RK's
political views alienated him, to some extent, from Burne-Jones
in his final years; but there were always ties of affection between
them, and RK was much saddened by his death.

Burne-Jones, Lady (née Georgiana Macdonald) (1840-1920),
married the distinguished Pre-Raphaelite painter Edward Burne-
Jones (1860). RK loved her, partly for her affectionate nature, partly
because her homes (first at the Grange, North End Road, London,
and later in Rottingdean) were always generously open to him and
to Carrie. Aunt Georgie was responsible for the arrangements of the
marriage of RK's parents; helped to slap life into Trix, RK's sister,
shortly after her troubled birth into the world; and, among many
acts of kindness and good judgement, was responsible for the
salvaging of 'Recessional' (Sarah Norton had recovered the scrap
of paper from RK's wastebasket, but RK insisted that Aunt Georgie
decide whether it should be saved for revision and publication).

Burne-Jones, Philip (1861–1926), son of Georgiana and Sir Edward Burne-Jones, brother of the Margaret who married John W. Mackail, played as a child with RK at Rottingdean, during the latter's enforced separation from his parents. In the early 1890s Phil saw a good deal of RK in London. The most important intersection of their artistic interests took place in 1897, when RK wrote a poem to accompany Phil's painting *The Vampire*, which had been created partly to celebrate Mrs Patrick Campbell, the actress:

> A fool there was and he made his prayer
> (Even as you and I!)
> To a rag and a bone and a hank of hair
> (We called her the woman who did not care)
> But the fool he called her his lady fair –
> (Even as you and I . . . .)

The picture, exhibited at the New Gallery, created a sensation, and RK's verses instantly became notorious. The National Portrait Gallery today exhibits Phil's portrait of RK, painted in 1899.

Catlin, Mrs, who lived in Morristown, New Jersey, met the Kiplings on their voyage to Bermuda (1894), and enjoyed their company. In 1901 the Catlins and their two daughters visited the Kiplings, and took them to Paris for a short pleasant stay. The Kiplings visited – whenever they were touring France – the Château d'Annel, near Compiègne, where Chauncy Depew, who had married Julia Catlin, one of the daughters, maintained his residence. In September 1914, Mrs Catlin, a refugee, arrived at Bateman's with stories of German atrocities. After the war Julia married General Taufflieb, who had met RK during the First World War. The Kiplings were on their way to visit the Tauffliebs in Paris when RK, in London, was stricken with the illness that led to his death.

Conland, James (1851-1903), was the doctor who attended Carrie when she gave birth to Josephine (1892) in Brattleboro, Vermont, and who remained the family physician of the Kiplings during their American years. After the furnace-door mishap (1895), Dr Conland ordered Carrie to recuperate in a warmer climate; this prescription led to a six-week tour of Washington, DC, when RK made important contacts with the political life of the American capital. Dr Conland had been a fisherman, and his informed talk about fishermen on the Grand Banks was doubtless the major inspiration for the arduous research that RK undertook for the writing of *Captains Courageous*. (Some of the research was done with Dr Conland along as 'consultant'.) Dr Conland came to New York (1899) to take care of Josephine, but his efforts proved unavailing. Before completing the sale of his Vermont home to Mary Cabot, RK invited Dr Conland to pick what he wanted from his hunting and fishing gear.

Crofts, William Carr (1846–1912), was a major inspiration for the character of King in *Stalky & Co.* (He shared the honour with F.W. Haslam, who had taught Latin at an earlier time to RK.) The son of a barrister, Crofts attended Merton College and then Brasenose, Oxford, where he distinguished himself as a classical scholar and an oarsman. He took up a teaching-post at the United Services College in 1875, and four years later, as deputy head, he served as both Senior Classics Master and Senior Housemaster. RK portrays King as a stern disciplinarian, though his own love of Latin derived in important measure from a dictum of Crofts, 'Give a boy more work than he can do and he'll do it.'

De Forest, Lockwood (1850–1932), responded warmly and help-fully to a request made by JLK, who wrote from India, to introduce his son to people who might advance his professional career in the United States (1889). The two men had been friends in India. De Forest – on whom RK called – gave him a letter to Henry Harper; though this contact with a well-known publishing-firm did not immediately lead to a contract, the friendship between the two men proved enduring; RK and De Forest went fishing on the Gaspé Peninsula, Canada (1896). It was to the Manhattan home of a De Forest sister that Josephine, ill with fever in the New York hotel in which RK himself almost died, was removed, and it was there that she died.

Doubleday, Frank N. (1862–1934), offered Kipling during his Vermont years the chance to publish a complete edition of his works. Because of his initials (FND), the RK's nicknamed him 'Effendi', and enjoyed his company (unusual, in that RK, like all writers, had several reasons, during the 1890s, to regard publishers with suspicion). After Doubleday left Charles Scribner's Sons, he secured an agreement to publish all American editions of RK's works. He also proved a tower of strength at the time of RK's near-fatal illness in 1899; working under the directions of RK's doctors, he did a great deal to keep Carrie from sinking into depression. His hardest duty was telling RK that Josephine had died: 'I took a seat beside him and told the story in as few words as I could. He listened in silence till I had finished, then turned his face to the wall.'

Dufferin, Lord: *see* Frederick Blackwood.

Dunsterville, Major General Lionel Charles (1865-1946), was the son of Lieutenant General Lionel d'Arcy Dunsterville, and continued a notable family tradition of military service. He fought in Waziristan, the North-West Frontier region of India, and China, and in various sectors during the First World War. Perhaps his most important campaign was fought in north-west Persia and the Caucasus (1918). He is the original Stalky in *Stalky & Co.*, the fictionalised version of RK's years at the United Services College, Westward Ho! Dunsterville denied that he was as clever as RK made him out to be, and claimed only that he was 'one of the prevailing spirits of this most untypical school'. He was the unanimous choice to be the first person to hold the post of President of the Kipling Society, and he served in that capacity for almost two decades.

Fleming, Lieutenant Colonel J.M. (1858–1942), husband of Alice Macdonald Kipling (RK's sister), was the son of Surgeon-General Andrew Fleming of the Indian Army Medical Service. His military career began in 1879, when he received a commission in the King's Own Scottish Borderers. He retired in 1911, and wrote 'The ABC of the More Important Battles of the Eighteenth and Nineteenth Century'; the outbreak of the Second World War prevented its publication, although John Buchan, who read it in manuscript, approved it.

Frölich, Alfred (1871–1953), a doctor at the Neurological Institute at the University of Vienna, served as a consulting physician for the Kiplings during their visits to Switzerland. He first met RK in Engelberg on 28 December 1908 (the day of the great earthquake that destroyed Messina), and carried on an extensive correspondence until RK's death. Dr Frölich, at one fancy-dress ball, made himself up as RK, and entered the ballroom with Carrie on his arm. 'The ball guests, on seeing two RK's, thought they were the victims of an illusion caused by the heady Christmas punch.'

Garrard, Violet ('Flo') (1856–1938), was the young woman to whom RK gave his heart – and by whom he was spurned. They met at Mrs Holloway's home in Southsea, when RK came to take Trix away (during the holidays of 1880). She, like RK in the years before his only return to Lorne Lodge, was a paying guest of the Holloways. He wrote a number of sentimental and romantic poems for her: *Sundry Phansies*. Before he went off to India and his 'seven years' hard', he proposed to her, and (despite the fact that we can never know what her response may have been) he believed himself engaged. This illusion lasted until the spring of 1884, when she wrote to him in Lahore, breaking the relationship. In February 1890, the two unexpectedly met on a London street, and RK's old passion rekindled. Two months later he visited her in Paris, where she shared a studio with a friend. Nothing came of his efforts to persuade her to take up the relationship on the old basis. Trix always thought of Flo as a chilly personality, and the evidence contained in Flo's sketch-book – complete with doodles by RK – does not indicate that she had a great artistic talent. She may have left her most permanent mark on his career by becoming the model for the character Maisie in *The Light that Failed*, but Trix also served as partial inspiration, and it is likely that Flo was the model only for the Maisie of the novel's second half.

Haggard, Sir Henry Rider (1856–1925) was educated at Ipswich Grammar School and by various private tutors. In the 1870s he served in various administrative capacities in the Transvaal, and, after deciding that the bar was not for him, he cultivated two strong passions, agricultural reform and the writing of romantic fiction. Notable publications in the first category are *The Farmer's Year Book* (1899), *Rural England* (2 vols, 1902), and *The Poor and the Land* (1905). In the second category must be listed such popular novels as *King Solomon's Mines* (1885), *She* (1887) and *Allan Quatermain* (1887). He reported on Salvation Army settlements in the United States, and travelled round the world (1912–17) as a member of the Dominions Royal Commission. In 1918 he served as a member of the Empire Settlement Committee. Haggard met RK in London in October 1889, probably at the Savile Club. RK was inspired to write the *Jungle Books* after reading Haggard's *Nada the Lily*, and he helped Haggard construct the plots of *The Ghost Kings, Allan and the Ice-Gods* and *Red Eve*. RK also provided extensive advice on the last of the *She* stories, *Wisdom's Daughter*. RK wrote long letters to Haggard during the painful three final months of Haggard's life. This probably was the closest and most professionally satisfying friendship of RK's middle years.

Henley, William Ernest (1849–1903), edited the *Scots Observer*, a widely read and quoted literary magazine of the 1890s; he was delighted to 'discover' RK. Beginning in February 1890, with the publication of 'Tommy', 'Fuzzy-Wuzzy', 'Loot', 'The Widow at Windsor', 'Gunga Din' and 'Mandalay', right through June, Henley fostered RK's career as a 'coming young man'. When he visited London, he invited RK to all his bachelor dinner-parties. His Tory politics were, in large measure, congenial to RK's own beliefs. In later years, though unwilling to allow others to call him one of Henley's protégés or disciples, RK spoke of him as 'kind, generous, and a jewel of an editor'. Henley's popular anthology *Lyra Heroica* (assembled for children) printed as its first poem one of RK's most striking ballads about the responsibilities of Englishmen overseas, 'The English Flag'. Henley often visited the Elms in Rottingdean; RK made a point of looking him up, whenever he could, in the late 1890s.

Hill, Edmonia (1858–1952), remembered how – in India – the fact of her Americanness first intrigued RK. She was a lively, friendly, intelligent critic of his writings, and he confided in her perhaps more of his intimate thoughts than he did any of his male friends. He called her by her nickname 'Ted', and she in turn supplied a number of usable details for his stories (such as the names for the characters in 'The Man Who Would Be King'). RK's biographer C. E. Carrington believes that 'On Greenhow Hill', which tells (among other things) of Learoyd's inability to satisfy the father of his sweetheart as to his religious orthodoxy, and his subsequent flight from Methodism, is thinly disguised autobiography. RK wrote 'love letters' to Caroline Taylor, Edmonia's younger sister, but the engagement – if it ever advanced to that stage – ran into trouble partly because of RK's theological opinions, which satisfied neither Caroline nor her father, a strict clergyman. A dignified and 'proper' tone in correspondence replaced personal contacts after Edmonia returned to the United States (Dec 1890). (See entry for Caroline Taylor.)

Hill, S. A., was a meteorologist working for the Indian Government, and held a professorship at Muir Central College, Allahabad, in the late 1880s. He and his wife met RK (1887) at a dinner-party given by the Allens (Sir George Allen owned both the *Civil and Military Gazette* and the *Pioneer*), and immediately struck up a firm friendship with him. RK, who liked both the Hills very much, was especially intrigued by Professor Hill's interests in photography. RK paid room and board while living with the Hills (1888–9), and wrote 'Baa Baa, Black Sheep' in their bungalow. Professor Hill and his wife enjoyed a visit from RK at their American home (Beaver, Pennsylvania). After Professor Hill had gone on ahead, RK accompanied Mrs Hill, Caroline Taylor and their cousin Edgar Taylor part-way on their return trip to India, and stopped off in England. Professor Hill died prematurely in India (1890).

Holloway, Pryse Agar (1810–74), known as 'Uncle Harry', was the son of Benjamin Holloway, 'gentleman' of Oxfordshire. He joined the Royal Navy in 1824; became a midshipman on *HMS Brisk* in 1825; and probably joined the Merchant Navy after leaving the *Brisk*. RK, who lived in his house at Southsea during some troubled and lonely years of childhood (see 'Baa Baa, Black Sheep', the opening pages of *Something of Myself*, and the childhood passages recorded in *The Light that Failed*), thought of him (mistakenly) as having achieved the rank of Captain. Holloway showed kindness, in various small ways, to RK, and sheltered him from the unpleasantness of his wife, Sarah. His son, Henry Thomas Holloway, acted as a bully, and tormented RK both physically and spiritually; RK called him 'the Devil-Boy'.

Holloway, Sarah, 'took in children whose parents were in India'. RK described her, years afterwards, as 'Aunty Rosa', and pictured her as cruel and narrow-minded. The question of how exaggerated RK's portrayal of her personality may have been probably can never be resolved, though the fact that she made Trix her favourite is undisputed by biographers. RK hated her Evangelical tirades, her punishments for trivial offences, and her lies (for example, that she had taken in the Kipling children out of pity). Trix, who resented what she considered to be the abandonment by her aunts of both Ruddy and herself, stayed in 'the House of Desolation' for several years after RK left for the United Services College, and, probably because Aunty Rosa (who had always wanted a daughter) made much of her, did not seem to cherish memories of Lorne Lodge anywhere near as grim as those sustained by her brother over a full lifetime.

James, Henry (1843–1916), was one of the sponsors of RK's election to the Savile Club (1890) within a year after his arrival in London. Thereafter James watched, warily, the developing career of a writer whose experiences in India were so exotic and remote that James hardly knew how to assess them. It was never a close relationship, though James did contribute a preface to *Mine Own People* (a book published in 1891 by J.W. Lovell to secure copyrights for a number of short stories, later to be entitled *Life's Handicap* because *Mine Own People* had been pre-empted), dined with RK in London, in Rottingdean and at Bateman's, and gave away the bride at RK's wedding. (The last event may be explained at least partly by James's admiration of Wolcott Balestier, and his continuing interest in the welfare of the Balestier family; he did not like Carrie, and wondered why RK had chosen her.) James's criticism of RK's fiction deepened as the 1890s wore on, and he wrote to Grace Norton (Christmas Day 1897) that RK's talent was 'quite diabolically great. . . . Almost nothing civilised save steam and patriotism . . . .' This, unfortunately, became a continuing refrain in James's public comments as well, and its tone influenced at least one generation of critics.

Jameson, Sir Leander Starr (1853–1917), is perhaps best remembered for 'Jameson's raid', which took place in late December 1895. This foredoomed invasion of the Transvaal by 450 men aimed to overthrow the Government of the South African Republic, but Jameson, who accepted full responsibility, was forced to surrender to the Boers at Doornkop, near Johannesburg, only a few days after the raid began. The consequences were serious; Jameson was tried in London for an offence against the Foreign Enlistment Act, and disgraced by a Holloway prison sentence.

The rest of his life was, nevertheless, as remarkable as what had preceded it; he became the Prime Minister of Cape Colony (1904), and probably did as much as any individual to help form the Union of South Africa. As the closest friend of Cecil John Rhodes from 1886 on, Jameson chose to be buried next to Rhodes in the Matoppo Hills, near Bulawayo. RK, who modelled 'If' on his conception of Jameson's character, admired Jameson as the man who would save South Africa from its internal schisms and from the excesses of those who would exploit its natural resources; after Jameson's grip on the reins of power loosened, RK lost his faith in the future of the land he had loved so well for two decades. It is significant that Jameson lost his majority in the election of 1907, and RK paid his last visit to the Woolsack in 1908. Jameson's sparkling and attractive personality was quite unlike that of the silent and somewhat dour Rhodes; but the two men, for 15 years, formed a powerful team.

Kipling, Alice ('Trix') (1868–1948), was a talented child, and no less inventive and lively than her brother RK. She probably suffered less than RK did during her Southsea years (1871–80), even though she stayed with Mrs Holloway several years longer than her brother did. She enjoyed her stay in India as a member of the 'Family Square' (her parents, RK and herself); she wrote poetry and, with RK, published *Echoes*. In 1885, she contributed to a family magazine called *Quartette*. She had one frustrated affair with the Viceroy's son, but finally settled on John Fleming, an officer in the Survey Department, and married him at the age of 21. The record of an ill-matched and quarrelling pair may be found in her novel *The Heart of a Maid* (1890). Suffering from periodic bouts of deep depression, Trix was nursed by her mother. After she discovered that she had psychic powers, she worked with the British Society of Psychical Research, London (1903–10). Her mental problems ended in the 1930s. After the death of her husband in 1942, she lived on to the age of 80 as a widow in Edinburgh.

Kipling, Alice Macdonald (1837–1910), RK's mother, was the daughter of George Browne Macdonald, a Wesleyan minister, and his wife Hannah. She was one of 11 children, and the oldest of the daughters; the other children were Mary, Henry (Harry), Caroline, Georgiana (who married Sir Edward Poynter, President of the Royal Academy), Louisa (who married Alfred Baldwin),

Walter, Edith and Herbert. A witty and beautiful woman with wide-ranging interests in literature, Alice encouraged her son in his professional objectives. She became famous in both Lahore and Simla as a hostess.

Kipling, Caroline ('Carrie', née Balestier) (1862–1939), was very proud of her family ancestry. Her grandfather, Joseph Balestier, was a wealthy lawyer of Brattleboro who left an estate of $600,000 when he died in 1888; her grandmother, Caroline Starr Wolcott Balestier, could trace her lineage back to a signer of the Declaration of Independence, and as a widow lived in grand style at her large farmhouse, named Beechwood. One of her sons, Henry, married Anna Smith, daughter of Judge Peshine Smith, who had an international reputation; their children included Wolcott, who made a deep impression on RK and became his closest friend; Caroline and Josephine (the latter being considered the more beautiful); and Beatty, whose quarrel with RK was ultimately to drive the Kiplings from their home in the United States permanently. Edmund Gosse took credit for introducing RK to Wolcott (see entry for Wolcott Balestier), and it is possible, as Charles Carrington, Kipling's biographer, surmises, that RK felt an obligation to take care of the family after Wolcott's unexpected death in Dresden (6 Dec 1891). At any rate, RK's parents were not enthusiastic about the marriage, and Henry James, in a letter to his brother William (6 Feb 1892), called her 'a hard devoted capable little person whom I don't in the least understand his marrying'. Nevertheless, there was genuine affection on both sides, and complete loyalty throughout the 44 years of marriage that followed. She was particularly effective in managing RK's business affairs and shielding him from unwanted visitors. RK once told J.H.C. Brooking that he thought of himself as the Works, and Carrie as the Works Manager 'when business decisions were required'. Opinions of Carrie's personality have been mixed. Lady Milner stressed her liveliness and wit, but others resented her bossiness and occasional sharpness of tongue. All agree, however, that the double family tragedy of Josephine and John's deaths darkened her life and aggravated a series of illnesses in her last two decades.

Kipling, Elsie (Mrs George Bambridge) (1896–1976), daughter of RK, was born in Brattleboro, Vermont, only a few months before her parents left their home at Naulakha. The second version of the 'Family Square' consisted of her, her parents and her brother John. (She is a major character in the stories 'Gloriana' and 'Marklake Witches'.) Although John attended prep school and public school, Elsie was educated by governesses at Rottingdean and in South Africa. Like her parents, she was deeply shocked by John's death, and Bateman's – after 1915 – often seemed like a house of gloom. She enjoyed the friendship of Lady Edward Cecil (afterwards Lady Milner). Her marriage to George Bambridge, a diplomatic attaché at Madrid (and formerly a fellow ensign with John in the Irish Guards), meant that Bateman's became even lonelier for her parents. RK financed the purchase of Wimpole Hall, and George, who had left the diplomatic service, became a landowner (the estate covered 2000 acres). After George's death from pneumonia in 1943, Elsie lived, childless, for 30 years at Wimpole Hall. Her final years were spent in poor health; her memory sometimes failed; but she was always a zealous guardian of her father's reputation.

Kipling, John (1897–1915), RK's son, was born at Rottingdean, and at first seemed destined for a bright career. Admiral of the Fleet Sir John Fisher wanted to nominate him for a naval cadetship; poor eyesight (something he shared with his father) prevented him from moving in that direction. He attended Wellington College, Berkshire, a public school with a strong military tradition. His academic record was not distinguished, but his personality was cheerful and earned him many friendships. At first rejected for military duty after the outbreak of war in 1914, he tried again, this time with the sponsorship of Field Marshal Lord Roberts, Colonel-in-Chief of the Irish Guards, and secured a commission in that regiment. (His father's appeal to Lord Roberts to assist the young man was the deciding factor.) In August 1915 he was sent to France in the Second Battalion, and died in the Battle of Loos. In 1935 RK set up an endowment so that 'The Last Post' would be blown each night at Loos.

Kipling, John Lockwood (1837–1911), Kipling's father, was the son of the Rev Joseph Kipling (a Methodist) and Frances Lockwood (described by RK as 'an old-fashioned Puritan Saint with a face like a chaste cameo'). JLK studied practical arts (modelling, design) at the Stoke-on-Trent School of Art. He worked for seven years at a Staffordshire pottery, and then moved to London, where he became an architectural sculptor. He was responsible for most of the modelling for the terracotta decorations of the Department of Science and Art in the Museum at South Kensington. He married Alice Macdonald after a three-year courtship, and took her to India, where he became (at the Sir James Jeejeebhoy School of Art and Industry) a teacher, and later an administrator, first in Bombay and later Lahore. His major publication was *Beast and Man in India*, but he completed several important art commissions and often contributed illustrations to his son's books. He served as a 'literary consultant' to RK's writings, and his advice was highly valued by his son.

Kipling, Josephine (1892–9) was born in Brattleboro, Vermont, and died in New York. Her brief life was a great joy to both parents, but particularly RK, who wrote the *Just So Stories* for her even more than for John. (See Angela Thirkell's *Three Houses*, 1931, for a delightful description of how RK read the stories aloud to his children.) RK also began a lifelong friendship with Dr James Conland, who delivered Josephine. But Josephine's vivacity, intelligence and beauty were so striking that, on learning of her death (an event that occurred while he was dangerously ill in New York City), RK was devastated. As Elsie Bambridge wrote, in a memoir contributed to C.E. Carrington's life of RK, 'There is no doubt that little Josephine had been his greatest joy during her short life. . . . She belonged to his early, happy days, and his life was never the same after her death; a light had gone out that could never be rekindled.' The short story 'They' expresses, in poignant terms, his undying affection for a daughter so tragically taken from him.

Landon, Perceval (1869–1927) led a hectic life as a journalist. He went with Younghusband to Lhasa (1904), and fulfilled many arduous, even dangerous, missions in the East for both *The Times* and the *Daily Telegraph*. He met RK in Cape Town during the Boer War, and later collaborated with RK on *The Friend* (Bloemfontein). RK was pleased to have him stay as a visitor in a cottage (Keylands) on the Bateman's estate whenever he visited. The two men enjoyed each other's company during tours of the French and Italian fronts in 1915 and 1917. (RK's *France at War* and *The War in the Mountains* record their experiences together.)

Lang, Andrew (1844–1912), responded very negatively to Kipling's short story 'The Mark of the Beast', which had been sent to him in manuscript form. Shortly thereafter, he changed his mind; *Departmental Ditties* – sent out from India to London – convinced him that RK was a budding genius. He wrote to RK, and helped make the possibility of literary success in England an attractive vision to RK, who was completing 'seven years' hard' as a journalist. Lang also reviewed *Plain Tales from the Hills* for the *Daily News*, and wrote an important article for *Harper's Weekly* (30 Aug 1890) that praised RK's work with generosity and warmth. Lang acted as one of RK's sponsors at the Savile Club shortly after his arrival in London.

Ley, Mary (née Walford) (1899–1982), served as secretary to RK from 1927 to 1931, and later as companion and secretary to the recently widowed Elsie Bambridge (1943). She lived at Wimpole Hall until she married Dr Henry Ley, a cathedral organist. She was one of the first women graduates of Oxford, reading English. Cecily Nicholson succeeded her as RK's private secretary.

Macdonald, Agnes (1843–1906), married to Edward Poynter (1836–1919), who was a mover and a shaker in the Royal Academy, serving for 20 years as its president. 'Aunt Aggie', as RK called her, helped to introduce RK to fashionable society after his return to London in 1889. The Poynters maintained close relationships with the Burne-Joneses.

Macdonald, Florence, daughter of the Rev Frederick Macdonald, and RK's cousin, delighted, along with her five siblings, in RK's mischief-making (it frequently got them all into trouble). In later years she became convinced of his great insights into feminine psychology, children and animals. RK frequently read his current stories to her. One of his remarks that she recorded is of special interest. Referring to 'Recessional', he said that, when one has three generations of Methody ministers behind one, 'the pulpit streak is bound to show'. She died in January 1956.

Macdonald, Frederick (1842–1928), was AMK's brother and a young Methodist minister at Burslem. He accompanied her to the picnic party at which she met JLK. He was regarded by his sisters as the intellectual member of the family because of his wide-ranging reading and love of the arts. He accompanied RK to the United States (1891), but gave away the game of RK's incognito by answering candidly the questions of reporters who met them at the dock. RK, in disgust, returned to England (the ostensible reason for his visit, renewing acquaintance with his uncle Henry, disintegrated when he and Uncle Fred learned that Henry had died while they were crossing the Atlantic). Perhaps nothing RK did impressed his uncle more than the writing of 'Recessional', which (he told RK) had 'touched' the entire community – that is to say, the Macdonald family.

Macdonald, George Browne (1805–68), grandfather of RK, was a famous Wesleyan preacher. His ministry at various London churches began in 1825, and lasted until his death. His wife Hannah Jones gave him 11 children, and four of his daughters – all of them beautiful and witty – married extremely well. RK's antics as a very young child on a brief visit to England upset him; he was ailing, and 'Ruddy' made an unconscionable amount of noise and fuss.

Macdonald, Hannah Jones (1809–75) was the daughter of John Jones of Manchester. She married the Rev George Browne Macdonald, and produced several handsome and beautiful children whose marriages created veritable dynasties of successful artists and politicians. Yet she suffered from fits of melancholia, and wanted the lives of her daughters to be 'fuller, more complete' than her own. Her Wesleyan faith, over-rigorously interpreted, may have produced a continuing strain of tension in AMK, the mother of RK. She probably believed that Mrs Holloway's discipline at Lorne Lodge, Southsea, was beneficial.

Mackail, John William (1859–1945), distinguished translator, don, literary critic and biographer (e.g. of William Morris), was the husband of Margaret Burne-Jones, the only daughter of Sir Edward Burne-Jones, and the father of Denis Mackail, a novelist. His elder daughter, Angela Thirkell, has written charmingly about her memories of RK (in *Three Houses*, 1931). Professor Mackail was liberal in his political sympathies, and RK, irritated by opinions that he fought in the public prints, was often no less unforgiving in his personal relationships; he broke off his correspondence with Margaret as a consequence of her marriage, arguments over the Boer War, and the rising star of Fabian Socialism (in which both Mackails believed). RK took special umbrage at Mackail's statement, after 'Recessional' was published, that England was 'saving up for the most tremendous smash ever recorded in history if she does not look to her goings', and he wrote to him, 'The big smash is coming one of these days, sure enough but I think we shall pull through not without credit. It will be common people – the 3rd class carriages – that'll save us.'

Milner, Sir Alfred Milner, 1st Viscount (1854–1925), was, along with Jameson and Rhodes, a decisive figure in South African history. Kipling called him a 'silent capable man worrying out his path alone, down south, in the face of all conceivable discouragements', and placed faith in his administrative abilities to rectify the damage done by the Boer War. The Liberals won in a landslide in 1906, however, and the House of Commons vengefully voted a formal censure against Lord Milner (partly for his encouragement of a scheme to suspend the Cape constitution, partly for his plan to import Chinese labourers to work the mines of South Africa). Kipling, outraged, became convinced that the Boer War had been fought in vain, and he never forgave Winston Churchill, who at the time was Under Secretary of State for the Colonies. Lady Milner asked him, in 1925, to write the life of her husband, who had just died; but Kipling, heartsick over the evolving history of a nation that he felt had been betrayed, refused, and indeed resigned from the Rhodes Trust less than a month later.

Moreau, Émile Edouard (1856–1937), met RK at the Club in Allahabad, and frequently played poker with him. As the senior partner of A. G. Wheeler and Co., the company that controlled the railway bookstalls in India, he recognised RK's talents as eminently suited to the vastly expanded reading-public of both India and England. He proposed to circulate more widely the six volumes that RK had already published in the Indian Railway Library, and to underwrite all costs in exchange for royalties. These stories were reprinted in England by Sampson, Low, Marston and Co., and attracted the reviews of responsible critics (Andrew Lang and Oscar Wilde, among others).

Morris, William (1834–96), known as 'Uncle Topsy', touched RK's life at several points during his childhood. He was a boisterous teller of tales, and sometimes used children (including RK) as his audience; RK decorated his study at the United Services College after the aesthetic style popularised by William Morris; but when the adult RK saw, close up, the 'Merry England' socialism of Morris, he did not like its sweeping attack on imperial concepts of administration in the overseas colonies and dominions.

Nicholson, Cecily (1900–82), was RK's last private secretary, and stayed at Bateman's from 1932 to 1940; she moved to Wimpole Hall to assist Mrs Bambridge, RK's daughter, between 1949 and 1954. Her grandfather, father and four uncles served with distinction in various military and naval campaigns. She believed in being discreet about her employers, and her memoirs, published in the *Kipling Journal* (1980–2), offer few revelations.

Norton, Charles Eliot (1827–1908), remained a close friend of the RKs in the United States even after the bitter events in Vermont and New York that terminated RK's willingness to visit the country. Norton was a New England critic, and a Harvard professor of international standing who taught the history of art (1875–98). RK ranked him with JLK and his uncle as major formative influences (i.e. mentors). Norton had visited India, and sympathised with RK's views on the obligations of imperial administrators. RK played with Sallie Norton at North End Road, and, after Naulakha was built, the Kiplings frequently visited the Nortons at Ashfield, Massachusetts. Although Norton later was unhappy with RK's views on both the Spanish-American War and the Boer War as being too extreme, he filled an important niche in RK's life, and no biographer of RK can afford to ignore the lengthy correspondence between the two men.

Osler, Sir William (1849–1919), Canadian-born, was one of the most eminent doctors of the late Victorian and Edwardian ages. A resident of Oxford from 1905 on, Osler was greatly impressed by Kipling's attitudes toward the responsibilities of empire, the need for honest and dignified work, and the sentiments expressed in 'If'. For the Encaenia at Oxford in 1907, the occasion on which RK received his honorary D. Litt., the Kiplings stayed with the Oslers; other occasions affording the opportunity for both to enjoy each other's company included meetings at the Athenaeum and at 'The Club' (which met each fortnight at Princes Hotel, Jermyn Street). John Kipling's death at Loos (1915) and Revere Osler's death at Ypres (1917) gave the two a melancholy bond as well. Osler's lifelong interest in the history of medicine influenced RK's descriptions of René Théophile Hyacinthe Laënnec, inventor of the stethoscope, in 'Marklake Witches', and of Nicholas Culpepper, the physician–astrologer in 'A Doctor of Medicine'; both stories are collected in *Rewards and Fairies*.

Ponton, Dorothy, at first a teacher of the Kipling children, became RK's private secretary (1919–24) and a live-in member of the family (until 1936).

Poynter, Ambrose (Sir Ambrose Macdonald Poynter, Bart.) (1867–1923), was the son of Agnes Macdonald Poynter, the sister of AMK (RK's mother). He wanted to be a writer; RK patiently listened to him read his poetry, which he could not sell to periodicals. He stood for RK at the wedding to Carrie, and in general RK much preferred his company to that of many members of the Savile Club. He suggested to RK the idea of a Roman centurion telling stories about his adventures to young children; RK developed the concept as *Puck of Pook's Hill*.

Poynter, Sir Edward John (1836–1919), who married Agnes Macdonald in 1866, was admired for his skilled academic draughtsmanship. He served for 20 years as President of the Royal Academy, after holding, at various times, such powerful posts as Principal of the National Art Training School, honorary secretary of a society to prevent the destruction of Egyptian monuments, and the directorship of the National Gallery. RK often attended banquets of the Royal Academy as his uncle's guest.

Price, Cormell (1836–1910), known as 'Uncle Crom', was educated at King Edward's School, Birmingham, where he enjoyed a firm friendship with Edward Burne-Jones. In 1854 he won an Open Scholarship to Brasenose College, Oxford, and developed ties with William Morris (a fellow-member of 'The Set', later called 'The Brotherhood') and Harry Macdonald, brother of the four Macdonald sisters. Deterred from pursuing a career that might lead either to holy orders or to medicine, Price, who entertained strong interests in Pre-Raphaelite art, literature, and social issues, took as his first full-time employment a position as a tutor in Russia to the son of a Russian count. This unsatisfactory position lasted for three years; he prepared several translations of Russian literary works. In 1863 he became Head of the Modern Side at the recently established Haileybury College; 11 years later he became the first headmaster at United Services College, Westward Ho! In 20 years he watched over 1014 boys, including RK, whose literary aspirations he encouraged. Four of his pupils won the Victoria Cross; more than 90 were admitted to the Distinguished Service Order.

Rattigan, Sir William (1842–1904), was a successful lawyer in Lahore who was part owner of the successful and influential *Civil and Military Gazette*. He, along with his co-owner James Walker, bought a controlling interest in the larger publishing-venture the *Pioneer* of Allahabad, which was widely regarded as the semi-official voice of the Punjab. According to Clive Rattigan, his son, JLK had 'induced' his father and Walker to give RK a job on the *Gazette*. (Clive edited both the *Gazette* and the *Pioneer*.) There is a striking resemblance between William Rattigan's life and the life of Kimball O'Hara in *Kim*: he was the son of an illiterate Irish private in the Ordnance Department of the East India Company. Nevertheless, RK had little or nothing to do with him personally.

Rhodes, Cecil John (1853–1902), met RK shortly after he was elected to the Athenaeum as its youngest member (1897); they dined with Alfred Milner. The relationship prospered, partly because Rhodes liked Carrie's company (ordinarily he was uncomfortable with women who wanted to talk about serious topics), partly because he enjoyed discussing with RK his vision of a South Africa working on English principles. Rhodes asked RK (1898), 'What is your dream?' and RK's answer, that Rhodes was part of it, pleased the older man. During the Boer War RK was delighted to hear of Rhodes's release from the siege of Kimberley, and made a lengthy trip to see him; he often travelled with Rhodes round his estates. Rhodes arranged for RK to make a trip through the territory of Rhodesia (Mar 1898). He also built for the Kiplings the Woolsack, adjoining his own estate, Groote Schuur, and it became their abode during their visits to the Cape for the next seven years. The Kiplings advised Rhodes on the terms whereby young men would be selected by the Rhodes Trust for financial assistance at Oxford. After Rhodes's death, RK was called on for advice about the will, and he wrote the memorial inscription for Rhodes's memorial:

> The immense and brooding Spirit still
> Shall quicken and control.
> Living he was the land, and dead,
> His soul shall be her soul!

Rimington, General Joseph Cameron (1864–1942), was a student at the United Services College during the heyday of the Stalky trio, and at one time shared a study with RK. He admired RK's literary skills as the editor of the school *Chronicle*. Rimington later served in the Royal Engineers in Burma, Mesopotamia and India.

Roberts, Frederick Sleigh Roberts, 1st Earl (1832–1914), served as Commander-in-Chief in India from 1885 to 1893, and RK, from the very beginning much impressed by his empathy with ordinary soldiers, wrote frequently about 'Bobs' as the sort of commander needed by the British Army all over the world. Howard Hensman, who represented the *Pioneer* in Simla, was a confidant of Lord Roberts, and his enhanced prestige made it easier for RK to perform his journalistic duties in both Lahore and Allahabad. Although RK had some sharply critical things to say about Lord Roberts's administrative talents (or failings), the two men developed a pleasant relationship; RK praised Bobs in some widely quoted verses; and they met again, frequently, during the Boer War, in which Lord Roberts served as Commander-in-Chief. RK strenuously supported Lord Roberts's schemes for conscription (particularly as embodied in the National Service League). One last service performed by Lord Roberts was the procuring of a Commission for John Kipling in the Irish Guards, his own regiment. Lord Roberts died at St-Omer, France, on 14 November 1914, on active service, 'as he would have wished' (*DNB*); RK wrote an elegy, 'Roberts, 1914'.

Robinson, E. Kay (1854–1928), met RK in 1886, very soon after he came out to India to work as assistant editor on the *Pioneer*, Allahabad. Signing verses published in the *Pioneer* with the initials 'KR' led to understandable misattributions, and RK, trying to clear up the problem, initiated a correspondence that soon blossomed into a friendship. While on leave, Robinson met RK's parents in Lahore. On his appointment as Editor of the *Civil and Military Gazette*, in place of Stephen Wheeler, he was charged by the owners to 'put some sparkle into the paper'. To do this, he gave freer rein to RK's talents; encouraged the writing of verse; and published 'turn-overs', which ultimately became the nucleus of *Plain Tales from the Hills*. Robinson's faith in RK's abilities led him to send eight copies of *Departmental Ditties* to English publishers, 'with recommendatory letters', and he urged RK to go to England to establish himself personally as a new force in English letters. Robinson's amusing description of an ink-splattered RK at work in the offices of the *Gazette* is a classic of reporting in its own right.

Roosevelt, Theodore (1858–1919), first met RK in 1895, when he was serving as Head of the Civil Service Commission in Washington, DC. Roosevelt enjoyed twisting the lion's tail, and told RK that he intended to use scare tactics (denouncing a treacherous Britain) in order to persuade Congress to put up more money for an expanded Navy. They enjoyed visiting the zoo together. After 1895, they corresponded with complete candour in the expressions of their views. When RK sent 'The White Man's Burden' to Roosevelt (Nov 1899), the American, while holding reservations about its worth as a poem, wrote to Henry Cabot Lodge that it made 'good sense from the expansionist standpoint'. The Spanish–American war, the occupation by the US military of the Philippines, and a subsequent bloody revolt in Luzon, helped to identify Roosevelt firmly with the tag in the popular imagination. RK and Roosevelt shared a low opinion of Woodrow Wilson as a human being, and his policy of neutrality in the first two years of the First World War aroused their contempt for him as a US President. When Roosevelt died, RK lamented the passing of 'Great Heart'.

Taylor, Caroline, younger sister of Edmonia Hill, did not meet RK until he visited Beaver, Pennsylvania, while travelling from India to England (1889). Her optimistic and lively temperament appealed to RK, and – as in the case of Flo Garrard – he thought he had fallen in love with her, though the promise of a happy future was most unlikely. Her father was a Methodist minister who disapproved of RK's religious creed (as defined by RK in a letter to Caroline, dated 9 Dec 1889). The engagement was broken off; when he met Trix in London early in 1890, he was still emotionally upset. Caroline returned to the United States with her father, and RK did not continue his correspondence with her. (See entry for Edmonia Hill.)

Walker, Sir James (1845–1927), a banker, organised a successful transportation system between Simla and the Plains. He was co-owner with Sir William Rattigan of both the *Civil and Military Gazette* and the *Pioneer*; he acted as RK's patron, giving the young man his first full-time job (at the request of his friends JLK and AMK), and provided lodging for RK whenever he visited Simla. RK once wrote that he owed his start in life to Walker.

Wallace, Edgar (1875–1932), a well-loved Fleet Street 'character', journalist, novelist and script-writer, went to South Africa as a private soldier in the Medical Staff Corps, Simonstown. He wrote – for the *Cape Times* – an ambitious poem, 'Welcome to Kipling', in the voice of 'a common Tommy'. RK, who met him six weeks later (Feb 1898), liked him, and offered advice to a would-be journalist: 'For God's sake, don't take to literature as a profession. Literature is a splendid mistress, but a bad wife!' Wallace became a war correspondent for Alfred Harmsworth's *Daily Mail*, replacing Julian Ralph, and 'scooped' his fellow correspondents on the signing of the peace treaty (1 June 1902). RK sent several of Wallace's books as light reading to the ailing King George V (1929).

Watt, A. P., the literary agent who took over Kipling's tangled copyrights, permissions problems, and serial and syndicate legalities, encountered some minor difficulties from the competitive Wolcott Balestier in 1890. Watt believed, for example, that a better deal on the American rights of *The Light that Failed* could have been secured; but Balestier's ebullient personality so appealed to Kipling that he proceeded without due caution. The controversy was rendered moot by Balestier's death in Dresden. 'Aleck' was more than an agent, of course; he sailed from England to New York in order to comfort Kipling during his near-fatal illness (1899), and he frequently visited Kipling in Sussex. 'I tried to read "God of our fathers" aloud this morning at home,' he wrote to Kipling, 'but I broke down.' Kipling, very close to the end of his unsuccessfully, after the writer had been rushed to Middlesex Hospital; internal bleeding from a perforated ulcer had gone too far. Webb-Johnson served in important posts in Manchester and London; was surgeon to Queen Mary; significantly expanded the activities of the Royal College of Surgeons; and, among numerous administrative posts, acted as President of the Royal Benevolent Medical Fund and president of the Royal Society of Medicine (1950–2). A patron of the arts, he was also a director of the Savoy Theatre, a good friend of RK, and an authority on the Bible and Shakespeare.

Wheeler, Stephen (1854–1937), was RK's editor (and half the white editorial staff) at the *Civil and Military Gazette* between 1882 and 1887. The two men first met during RK's school holidays (Easter 1882); Wheeler thought that the 16-year-old boy might do many of the prosaic tasks in the office. Wheeler's illness soon after RK arrived in Lahore (he was involved in a carriage accident) threw RK on his own resources; after a return to full-time duty, Wheeler put to use RK's skill at précis-writing and his knowledge of French. RK was assigned the task of writing up translations of all French reports on activity in Afghanistan and the North-West Frontier. Late in 1886 Wheeler, in ill health, returned to England. A few years later he introduced RK to Sidney Low, Editor of the *St James's Gazette*, the periodical on which he was working at the time. Wheeler and RK did not get along too well, and RK found Wheeler's successor, E. Kay Robinson, much more to his liking; but the apprenticeship that Wheeler forced him to serve was (RK believed) beneficial in almost every way to his future development as a professional writer.

Orel: *A Kipling Chronology*

Erratum

The following lines have been omitted from the bottom of page 104:

'...life could remember no serious difference between himself and Watt over a period of forty years.

Webb-Johnson, Alfred Edward (Baron Webb-Johnson) (1880–1958), the distinguished urologist and surgeon who operated on Kipling,...'

Select Bibliography

My compilation of important dates and events in Rudyard Kipling's chronology has benefited greatly from the testimony provided by contributors to the *Kipling Journal*, the official publication of the Kipling Society since March 1927. In hundreds of articles, transcripts of speeches, records of meetings, memoirs, and so on, members of Kipling's circle of friends, historians, researchers, admirers – and sometimes unfriendly critics – of Kipling's life and character have given us an extraordinary record of what is known and knowable about Kipling. The materials, however, are an *olla podrida*, and the need for a comprehensive index, more complete than the ones already assembled by members of the Society, remains strong.

There exists invaluable information, also, in the more than 5000 pages of *The Reader's Guide to Rudyard Kipling's Work*, prepared in eight volumes by Roger Lancelyn Green, Alec Mason and R. E. Harbord between 1961 and 1972 (Canterbury: Gibbs and Sons; later, Bournemouth: Boscombe Printers). The biographies of Charles Carrington, Angus Wilson and Lord Birkenhead, and the bibliography of secondary materials that was compiled and edited by Helmut E. Gerber and Edward Lauterbach, published in *English Fiction in Transition*, III, nos 3–5 (1960), and VIII, nos 3–4 (1965), have proved helpful. The most up-to-date review of where one may find Kipling manuscripts and collections of Kipling materials is Thomas Pinney's 'Kipling in the Libraries', *English Literature in Transition*, no. 29 (1986).

Because a knowledge of Kipling's life is crucial to any assessment of Kipling's art, critics who discuss Kipling almost invariably use biographical data. It has not been deemed possible, in the bibliography that follows, to separate the available secondary literature into mutually exclusive categories. The bibliographies of Kipling material are listed here because they often print important biographical information.

Unless otherwise indicated, the place of publication of the works listed is London.

Adams, Francis, *Essay in Modernity* (1899).
Amis, Kingsley, *Rudyard Kipling and his World* (1975).

Archer, William, *Poets of the Younger Generation* (1910).

Beresford, G. C., *Schooldays with Kipling* (1936).

Birkenhead, Lord, *Rudyard Kipling* (New York, 1987).

Bloom, Harold (ed.), *Rudyard Kipling* (New York, 1987).

Bodelsen, C. A., *Aspects of Kipling's Art* (1978).

Brown, C. Hilton, *Rudyard Kipling* (New York, 1945).

Carrington, Charles E., *Rudyard Kipling* (1955).

Chandler, Lloyd H., *A Summary of the Work of Rudyard Kipling* (New York, 1930).

Charles, Cecil, *Rudyard Kipling: The Man and his Work* (1899).

Chevrillon, André, *Rudyard Kipling* (Paris, 1936).

Cohen, Morton (ed.), *Rudyard Kipling to Rider Haggard: The Record of a Friendship* (1965).

Cornell, Louis L., *Kipling in India* (New York, 1966).

Croft-Cooke, Rupert, *Rudyard Kipling* (1948).

Dobrée, Bonamy, *The Lamp and the Lute* (1929).

——, *Rudyard Kipling* (1951).

——, *Rudyard Kipling: Realist and Fabulist* (1972).

Dunsterville, Lionel Charles, *Stalky's Reminiscences* (1928).

Durand, Ralph, *Handbook to the Poetry of Rudyard Kipling* (1914).

Eliot, T. S., *A Choice of Kipling's Verse* (1941).

Escarpit, Robert, *Rudyard Kipling: servitudes et grandeurs impériales* (Paris, 1955).

Falls, Cyril, *Rudyard Kipling: A Critical Study* (1951).

Fido, Martin, *Rudyard Kipling* (Feltham, Middx, 1974).

Gilbert, Elliot L., *The Good Kipling* (Athens, O., 1972).

—— (ed.), *Kipling and the Critics* (New York, 1965).

—— (ed.), *'O Beloved Kids': Rudyard Kipling's Letters to his Children (1906–15)* (1913).

Green, Roger Lancelyn, *Kipling and the Children* (1965).

—— (ed.), *Kipling: The Critical Heritage* (New York, 1971).

Gross, John, (ed.), *Rudyard Kipling: The Man, his Work, and his World* (1972).

Henn, T. R., *Kipling* (1967).

Husain, S. S., *Kipling and India* (Dacca, 1964).

Islam, Shamsul, *Kipling's 'Law': A Study of his Philosophy of Life* (1975).

Jackson, Holbrook, *The Eighteen-Nineties* (1913).

Knowles, F. L., *A Kipling Primer* (1900).

Lascelles, Mary, *The Story-Teller Retrieves the Past* (Oxford, 1980).

Le Gallienne, Richard, *Rudyard Kipling: A Criticism* (1900).

Livingston, Flora V., *Bibliography of the Works of Rudyard Kipling* (New York, 1927).

——, *Supplement to Bibliography of the Works of Rudyard Kipling* (Cambridge, Mass., 1938).

Martindell, E. W., *A Bibliography of the Works of Rudyard Kipling, 1881–1921* (1922).

Mason, Philip, *Kipling: The Glass, the Shadow, and the Fire* (1975).

McClure, John A., *Kipling and Conrad* (Cambridge, Mass., 1981).

Mertner, Edgar, *Rudyard Kipling und Seine Kritiker* (Darmstadt, 1983).

Moore, Gilbert, B. J., *Kipling and 'Orientalism'* (1986).

Moore, Katharine, *Kipling and the White Man's Burden* (1968).

Moss, Robert, F., *Rudyard Kipling and the Fiction of Adolescence* (1982).

Munson, Arnley, *Kipling's India* (1916).

Orel, Harold (ed.), *Kipling: Interviews and Recollections*, 2 vols (1983).

Orwell, George, *Dickens, Dali and Others* (New York, 1946).

Page, Norman, *A Kipling Companion* (1984).

Palmer, John, *Rudyard Kipling* (1985).

Pinney, Thomas (ed.), *Kipling's India: Uncollected Sketches* (1986).

Ponton, Dorothy, *Rudyard Kipling at Home and at Work* (Poole, 1953).

Rao, K. Bhaskara, *Rudyard Kipling's India* (Norman, Okla, 1967).

Rice, Howard, C., *Rudyard Kipling in New England* (Brattleboro, Vt, 1936).

Rossi, Matilde B., and Conoscitore, Clelia, *Fanciulli e adolescenti in Kipling* (Florence, 1969).

Rutherford, Angus (ed.), *Early Verse by Rudyard Kipling 1879–1889* (1986).

—— (ed.), *Kipling's Mind and Art* (Edinburgh and London, 1964).

Shahane, Vasant A., *Rudyard Kipling: Activist and Artist* (Carbondale and Edwardsville, Ill., 1973).

Shanks, Edward, *Rudyard Kipling: A Study in Literature and Political Ideas* (New York, 1940).

Smith, M. Van Wyk, *Drummer Hodge: The Poetry of the Anglo-Boer War* (Oxford, 1978).

Stewart, J. I. M., *Eight Modern Writers* (Oxford, 1963).

——, *Rudyard Kipling* (1986).

Stewart, James McG., *Rudyard Kipling: A Bibliographical Catalogue*, ed. A. W. Yeats (Toronto, 1959).

Sutcliff, Rosemary, *Rudyard Kipling*, (New York, 1961).

Thirkell, Angela, *Three Houses* (Oxford, 1931).

Tompkins, J. M. S., *The Art of Rudyard Kipling* (1959).

Trilling, Lionel, *The Liberal Imagination* (New York, 1951).

Water, Frederic, F. Van de, *Rudyard Kipling's Vermont Feud* (Weston, Vt, 1937).

Weygandt, A. M., *Kipling's Reading and its Influence on his Poetry* (Philadelphia, 1939).

Wilson, Angus, *The Strange Ride of Rudyard Kipling* (1977).

Wilson, Edmund, *The Wound and the Bow* (New York, 1959).

Young, W. Arthur, *A Dictionary of the Characters and Scenes in the Stories and Poems of Rudyard Kipling, 1886–1911* (1912); rev. J.H. McGivering and repr. as *A Kipling Dictionary* (1967).

Index

(Italic numbers refer to entries in the section 'Among Those Who Knew Kipling').